50¢

In appreciation of
your hospitality.

Alan & Joan Litchfield
23 Aug 98.

D1306999

GETTING
AHEAD BY
STAYING
BEHIND

GETTING AHEAD BY STAYING BEHIND

How to Be A Better Follower of Jesus

JOHN KRAMP

BROADMAN
&HOLMAN
PUBLISHERS

Nashville, Tennessee

(C) 1997
by John Kramp
All Rights Reserved
Printed in the United States

Published by Broadman & Holman Publishers, Nashville, Tennessee
Acquisitions & Development Editor: Vicki Crumpton
Interior Design: Desktop Miracles, Addison, Texas

4262-86
0-8054-6286-4

Dewey Decimal Classification: 248.84
Subject Heading: DISCIPLESHIP / CHRISTIAN LIFE
Library of Congress Card Catalog Number: 96-53017

Library of Congress Cataloging-in-Publication Data
Kramp, John, 1954–
    Getting ahead by staying behind : how to be a better follower of Jesus / John Kramp.
        p.   cm.
    Includes bibliographical references
    ISBN 0-8054-6286-4
    1. Christian life—Baptist authors. I: Title.
    BV4501.2.K686   1997
    248.4'861—dc21
                                                    96-53017
                                                    CIP

97 98 99 00 01   5 4 3 2 1

To Bill and Hellen Kramp
Absolutely the best

The Twenty-Four Followisms

1. You can learn a lot by following.
2. Anyone can follow.
3. Following is a simple process.
4. Following is important.
5. If you don't know the way, you should follow the leader.
6. Following begins with an initial choice.
7. Following requires focus.
8. Following requires continual adjustment to the leader.
9. Following builds relationship.
10. Following changes followers.
11. Followers go where their leaders are going.
12. If you're the follower, you're not the leader.
13. Followers always need their leaders.
14. People follow in different ways.
15. Sometimes it's hard to follow.
16. Testing while following enhances learning.
17. Those who fail can follow again.
18. You can follow the leader without seeing the leader.
19. You can follow the leader by following the leader's written directions.
20. You can follow the leader by listening to the leader's voice.
21. The better you know the leader, the easier it is to follow.
22. When it's dark, stand still and trust the leader.
23. You can help others follow as you follow the leader.
24. Following Jesus makes life meaningful.

Contents

Acknowledgments

Once again, many people have shared the process of writing this book with me.

Bill and Hellen Kramp, my parents, spent hours proofing rough copies of the manuscripts and offering suggestions for improvements. Without their efforts, I never would have completed this "night job" while keeping my "day job."

Lynn Marie, Courtney, and Kelly Kramp supported me throughout this process. Without their love, encouragement, and prayers, I never would have made it.

Roy Edgemon, my "boss" and friend, kept reminding me to keep my priorities straight and warned me about becoming too busy for the most important things. I'm fortunate to have him in my life.

Avery Willis has taught me about discipleship personally and through his courses, *MasterLife* and *MasterBuilder*. Without his influence, I would have struggled to write an article on discipleship, much less a book.

Mike Hyatt, my friend and literary agent, deserves the ultimate credit (or blame) for getting me involved in writing. Without him, *Out of Their Faces and Into Their Shoes* would still be rough notes in a file folder, and this book would not be a "second thought."

The folks at Broadman & Holman Publishers—Vicki Crumpton (my editor), Bucky Rosenbaum, Greg Webster, Susan Linklater, Colyer Robison, and others—believed in this project and continually encouraged me throughout the long writing process. I'm thankful for their skills and friendship.

John Kramp
April 1997

Followology 101

Followism 1:   You can learn a lot by following.

Followism 2:   Anyone can follow.

Followism 3:   Following is a simple process.

FOLLOWOLOGY 101

*You can learn a lot
by following.*

By the time you finish this book, you'll know how to use every "following" experience as a spiritual laboratory. When you follow directions, or follow a leader, or follow the car in front of you—in fact, every time you follow anyone, anywhere—you'll gain spiritual insights. That's Followology. Let's be honest, though. Studying following sounds sort of weird. At this point, it is not socially acceptable to tell people you are a followologist. Perhaps if I explain how I stumbled into this you'll understand why I am now an unapologetic followologist and why I hope you will become one too.

For me, it all began with Lostology. A few years ago I discovered how to find uncommon spiritual insights about evangelism in common physical experiences. If you read my book *Out of Their Faces and Into Their Shoes*, you already know how the process works and how to use your experiences of being physically lost to understand how secular people think and feel while they are spiritually lost. Just in case you haven't read that book, let me give you a fast-forward summary so you'll understand how all this fits together.

As the first, great lostologist, Jesus explained His mission on earth in the language of Lostology when He said, "For the Son of Man came to seek and to save what was lost" (Luke 19:10). Jesus used simple stories about a lost sheep, a lost coin, and a lost son to help people make a connection between ordinary experiences and spiritual truths. Through word pictures, Jesus helped people glimpse the value our Heavenly Father places on people who are spiritually lost. Jesus explained, "In the same way your Father in heaven is not willing that any of these little ones should be lost" (Matt. 18:14).

Jesus' mission on earth was a search-and-rescue operation with an unusual twist—in this case, the lost were in an enviable position. For Jesus, the term *lost* was not derogatory. Being lost implied there was some place you were supposed to be and someone who cared that you were not there. In contrast, if there was no place you were supposed to be and no one cared where you were, you could say you lacked direction or that you were lonesome, but you could not say you were lost. God changed all that. God declared that His creation was spiritually lost. In effect, God said, "You're supposed to be in a relationship with Me, but you're separated from Me. That means you are lost. And because you are lost, I will pay the ultimate price to rescue you." So Jesus, the great lostologist, completed the mission that made it possible for the lost to be found.

Even now our experiences of being physically lost can become living analogies that help us understand God's eternal plan to rescue the world and our responsibilities as part of His search-and-rescue-team. However, salvation (or "getting found") is only the first part of God's plan—like when friends jump out and yell, "Surprise!" at a birthday party. The surprise begins the party. So it is with Lostology. It helps us understand God's plan to find us, but in Followology we discover why we "get found."

If God's only goal was to rescue us, He could have zapped us straight to heaven once we became Christians so we could bypass the inevitable struggles of earth. But He didn't. He left us here—not forever, but for now. Obviously, something we do from the time we "get found" to the time we join Him in eternity is important. We "get found" so that we can follow. The process of following Jesus on earth changes us. That's why Jesus repeatedly gave a simple invitation during His earthly ministry: "Follow Me." That's why Jesus extends the same invitation to us today.

There is something intriguing about the simple idea that the Christian life has always centered on following Jesus—not just two thousand years ago, but today. Following says, "Jesus is here, active, and working in our world." Following says, "Jesus wants us to be with Him, to be part of what He is doing." But can our experiences of "following" in everyday life really help us follow Jesus as His disciples today? Let me use one of my "following" experiences to explain how Followology works and to help you begin to think like a followologist.

The Texas-to-Oregon Trail

When my family moved from Dallas, Texas, to Portland, Oregon, we ranked the challenge right up there with the Alaskan Iditarod dog-sled race. My children were young at the time, so I recruited my father, Bill, and my friend, Dean, to make the road trip with me. My wife, Lynn Marie, gladly volunteered to travel later by plane with our daughters.

On the January morning we left Dallas, a winter storm rolled across the country, icing roads and blowing snow. In spite of the weather, our three drivers prepared to face the rugged trail. We fired up our cars—the Blue Goose (our Olds Delta 88 for which the 100,000-mile mark was a dim memory) and Whitie (our vintage bottom-of-the-line Volvo with more than 60,000 miles). We checked our CB radios and winter weather supplies, waved to the well-wishers, and began our journey. My father (whom Dean affectionately dubbed "Big Bill" on the CB) took the lead in the Blue Goose. Dean and I followed in Whitie.

I am not good with directions. As a result, you may be surprised to learn that in spite of my navigational limitations, I faced the Texas-to-Oregon Trail adventure with absolute confidence.

You might guess that I was armed with a AAA bonus pack of highlighted maps that would guide us from Dallas to Portland. Wrong. I sneered at maps. You might expect that I had foolproof written directions. Wrong again. I scoffed at directions. My secret directional weapon was more potent than any map and more powerful than any set of directions. I had Big Bill.

As a connoisseur of road trips and a grand master of navigational strategy, Big Bill had assumed responsibility for our trek.

With skills honed through years of family vacations and international business travel, he prepared every detail of the daunting journey.

My personal plan was simple: follow Big Bill. Even for me, the logic was inescapable. There was no doubt that Big Bill was "The Way" to Portland. If I was in the car with him or at least kept him in sight from the other car, I would arrive in Portland also. All I had to do was follow him.

The Basics of Followology

Let's consider some principles of Followology we can draw from my experience of following Big Bill.

- *The roles were clear.* Big Bill was the leader; I was the follower.

- *The leader had the tough job.* Big Bill had to make the plans, monitor the maps, and make sure we arrived in Portland. I just had to make the trip.

- *The follower had to maintain contact with the leader.* Either visually or over the CB radio, I had to stay in contact with Big Bill. If I lost contact with him, I couldn't follow him.

- *The leader was "the way."* As long as I was in contact with Big Bill, I needed no other directions.

- *The follower had the opportunity to learn from the leader.* I had plenty of time during that trip to learn from Big Bill. Rather than just making the journey, I could learn the way. Then I could make that trip on my own in the future with confidence.

LOSTOLOGY TO FOLLOWOLOGY

Jesus emphasized the experience of following far more than the experience of being lost. But rather than telling parables about following, Jesus created living stories as He invited people to follow Him. Without ever using the term, Jesus introduced the concept of Followology and became the first great followologist. For our study, we'll use this simple definition:

Followology is the study of following and what that experience can teach Christians about discipleship.

The principles of Followology, added to those of Lostology, help us think about God's work in the world and in our lives in new ways— both with our minds and with our hearts. Yes, we were lost, but Jesus found us. Yet being found was not the end; it was the beginning. We were found so we could follow. And, as we will discover, following has always been a central part of God's plan for His people. To begin that story, though, we need to rewind the tape a few thousand years and peek in on one of the least promising collections of followers ever assembled. In the history of Followology, these folks were the ultimate slow group!

HELP FOR
THE SLOW GROUP

2

Anyone can follow.

Thanks to Sunday school lessons and the movie *The Ten Commandments*, most people know the basic story of the Israelites' exodus from Egypt. Unfortunately, many miss the key truth that can help them become better followers of Jesus today.

God knew the children of Israel would struggle to follow Him, so He implemented a unique follower-friendly system complete with visual aids. "By day the Lord went ahead of them in a pillar of cloud to guide them on their way and by night in a pillar of fire to give them light, so that they could travel by day or night. Neither the pillar of cloud by day nor the pillar of fire by night left its place in front of the people" (Exod. 13:21–22).

God made it possible for anyone, even a group of spiritual novices, to follow Him. He took the initiative. The process was incredibly simple.

What did the Israelites need to do every morning? Right. Check the status of the pillar of cloud. If it was moving, they knew God was ready for them to travel. If it was standing still, they knew God planned for them to stay put.

What was the last thing the Israelites did every night before they went to bed? They peeked from their tents to see what the pillar of fire was doing. If it was stationary, they knew God planned for them to spend the night where they were; but if it was moving, they peeled off pajamas, packed up their tents, and followed.

God's following system was clear-cut, mistake-proof, and tailor-made for everyone—including the slowest of the slow group. And everyone loved it. Well . . . not exactly.

7

THE IMAGI-NATION OF ISRAEL

The people *should* have loved God's "following" system, but they didn't. If you read through Exodus, Leviticus, Numbers, or Deuteronomy, you'll discover that the Israelites carped and whined about following God for forty years! Let's use our imaginations and envision what daily life might have been like for one Israelite family. Peek with me into a tattered tent at the far end of the Israelite camp, the portable desert home of a middle-aged couple named Herb and Louise. If you have a multimedia mind, you might imagine this couple looking like and sounding like Archie and Edith Bunker from the old television show "All In The Family."

Old Herb has had a tough week harvesting manna and plucking quail. So on this morning, he has decided to sleep in. From the depths of sound slumber, Herb is awakened by Louise's screechy voice.

"Herbie. Herbie! You'd better get up, Herbie." The sleep-fog swirls in Herb's mind, and Louise's voice mingles with the voices in his dream. The screech grows louder, accompanied by cold hands that are shaking him from side to side. "Herbie, you'd better get up," Louise says. "The cloud's moving again."

Herb opens one eye and looks up at Louise, curlers in her hair and wearing her pale pink bath robe with lavender pyramids on it. He grimaces, shudders, and then closes his eye and pulls the covers over his head. Louise responds by jerking all the covers off of him and scolding him. "Herbie, get out of this bed and start taking down the tent. We're going to be at the end of the line again and you know how unpleasant that is. Why, just the other day I was saying to Madel how I hate to be at the end because with all those animals you have to watch your step all day long and you can't visit with folks if you're always having to watch your step. I wish just for once we could get up closer to the front rather than always being at the end because—"

"Ssssh the noise, Louise," Herb says, interrupting Louise mid-phrase and then sitting up in bed. "I don't care if that cloud is moving or not. I don't care if that cloud is puffed up like the pharaoh's face in the sky. I'm staying right here. I've had it with this crazy schedule, and I'm not moving." And with that, Herb plops back on his bed.

Louise twists her handkerchief and sits down on the edge of the bed. "Don't talk that way, Herbie. I don't like it when you talk that way. You know what we're supposed to do. The cloud or the fire moves and then everybody starts following it. That's the way we do it. Everyone takes down their tents and then we all get in line. I know that sometimes your arthritis acts up because of all your quail plucking and you can't work very fast and that's why we're always at the back of the line, but I'd still like to be closer to the front. Just the other day, Madel was telling me that when the pillar moved time before last, they rushed and got at the front of the line right behind Moses' camel. Now I don't have to be that close because I don't care whose camel it is, it's no treat to be right behind it. But Herbie, I don't want to get left behind with you sleeping in your frog pajamas. Do you think that's a good idea? I really think you should get up and start taking down the tent because we're already going to be at the back, and if you don't—"

"Will you stuff a quail in it, Louise?" Herb says as he sits up on his bed in exasperation. "I'll tell you what I'm going to do, Louise. I'm going to make a deal with you. I'll get up. I'll pack up the tent. I'll load the camel. I'll even run to the very front of the line and tell Moses to wait for you. And Louise, all you have to do is one thing: don't say another word."

"Whatever you say, Herbie," Louise says as she pats him on the head and walks out the front of the tent.

LESSONS FROM THE SLOW GROUP

Some people think the story of the exodus wanderings is about the children of Israel, about people like Herb and Louise. But it's not; it's about God. Certainly, we can learn about human nature and even about ourselves by what we see in the Israelites. Yet we learn far more about God. In spite of their stiff-necked rebellion, God continued to guide the Israelites with the cloud and fire for the entire time they were in the desert. Even when they refused to fight for the promised land as He had commanded, God continued to lead them. Years later, Nehemiah marveled at God's grace. "Because of your great compassion you did not abandon them in the desert. By day the pillar of cloud did not cease to guide them on their path, nor the pillar of fire by night to shine on the way they were to take" (Neh. 9:19).

When Moses addressed the children of the exodus generation, he reminded them about God's gracious provision for them: "Remember how the LORD your God led you all the way in the desert these forty years, to humble you and to test you in order to know what was in your heart, whether or not you would keep his commands. He humbled you, causing you to hunger and then feeding you with manna, which neither you nor your fathers had known, to teach you that man does not live on bread alone but on every word that comes from the mouth of the LORD. Your clothes did not wear out and your feet did not swell during these forty years" (Deut. 8:2–4).

From the beginning, God has invited ordinary people to follow Him. The story of the children of Israel in the desert proves anyone can follow. Not because any of us are capable but because God is gracious. Spiritual following does not depend on us; it hinges on God. He extends the invitation and then enables us to respond.

We can, however, become better spiritual followers if we analyze the process and understand more about what God has invited us to do. Does that sound intimidating? It shouldn't. In fact, it reminds me of something my seventy-year-old neighbor, Manila, once told me about fishing. "When you're fishing," she said, "you're doing something. But not much."

Although fishing can be highly technical, require fancy equipment, and demand great skill, at the core, fishing is a simple process: bait a hook, attach a line, throw it in the water, and catch fish. Analyze the process and you will agree with my friend Manila—you're doing something, but not much. Although some people fish better than others, anyone can fish.

Following is the same thing. At the process level, following is simple. Although some people follow better than others, anyone can follow. Plus, here's the really good news: we can all become better followers—if we discover the secret. Interested? Psst! The secret is in the process.

JUST FOLLOW
THE FOLLOWING PROCESS

3

Following is a simple process.

Let's hone your Followology skills with a little story problem—just like the ones we all hated in high school. As the teachers used to say, "Don't be nervous. Simply do your best." Here we go:

Two cars (Car A and Car B) travel east on Interstate 40 toward Albuquerque, New Mexico. Car A proceeds with speeds as high as 85 mph and as low as 15 mph. No matter how fast or slow Car A travels, Car B remains behind Car A. The distance between Car A and Car B varies, from 15 yards to 100 yards, but at no time does Car B move ahead of Car A. Based on this information, describe the relationship between the driver in Car A and the driver in Car B. Choose the correct answer (or answers) from those listed below:

A. The driver of Car B is a secret fan of the driver in Car A.
B. The driver of Car A is an insecure male, obsessed by power, who is expressing pent-up hostility toward the driver of Car B by driving at erratic speeds.
C. The drivers of the two cars are married.
D. The driver of Car A is lost, but the driver of Car B is unaware of this fact.
E. The driver of Car B is trying desperately to pass Car A but has been unable to do so.
F. Car B is following Car A.
G. All of the above.
H. None of the above.

11

My overwhelming response to questions like this is thanksgiving that I no longer have to answer questions like this! Out of all my years of taking tests, I cannot recall a single question about following. No teacher asked me to analyze the relationship between the leader in Car A and the follower in Car B. No one asked me to analyze the principles that comprise the following process. What an oversight in our educational process. Lest you worry, let me assure you that we are about to compensate for this oversight by giving you a quick, analytical overview of following. Just imagine how your life will be enriched and how you will be able to amaze your friends once you know the seven principles of following. And even if you cannot fathom how you can drop these factual tidbits into after-dinner conversation, these concepts will be vital as you continue your study of Followology.

PRINCIPLES OF FOLLOWING

1. The Need Principle determines our *motivation* to follow.
2. The Choice Principle describes our *responsibility* in following.
3. The Focus Principle explains the basic *discipline* of following.
4. The Adjustment Principle affirms the *attitude* of a follower.
5. The Relationship Principle describes the *nature* of following.
6. The Change Principle explains the *purpose* of following.
7. The Destination Principle emphasizes the *reward* of following.

Of course, if you're one of those people who use acrostics to remember lists such as this, you can simply memorize the acronym NCFARCD and it will instantly remind you of each of the principles. For the rest of us, I'll simply explain each principle and illustrate it in the experience of the Israelites as they followed God through the wilderness. Later, in part 2 of our study, we'll probe each of these principles in detail and discover how each one helps us become better followers of Jesus today.

Principle #1: The Need
Our motivation for following is always in direct proportion to our awareness of our need. If we are convinced we know the way, we will not be interested in following. Self-confident and self-assured people make poor followers.

The Israelites, in contrast, recognized their need for a leader as they left Egypt and prepared to travel through the desert. Since their ancestors had been slaves for generations, the exodus created a huge problem. They had never been outside of Egypt, had never been where they wanted to go, and had no idea how to get there. So when God offered to lead them, their motivation to follow was high—at least initially.

Principle #2: The Choice

Motivation and choice are different. One can be motivated to do something without taking action, but nothing happens until someone makes an initial choice. Choice is the follower's basic responsibility.

So it was with the Israelites. They stood on the edge of the Red Sea, stuck between the proverbial rock and a hard place (in reality, a wet place). In front of them was water; behind them was the Egyptian army. They had limited options. So when God parted the Red Sea and made it possible for them to follow Moses across on dry ground, they had to make a choice: stay on the shore or walk through the water. Their choice required faith. They had no assurance that the unzipped sea would remain open. They simply had to trust the God who parted the waters to hold the waters.

The people chose to follow God and thereby began an incredible adventure. Later, the New Testament would compare their experience to being baptized. It was a memorable event, a once-in-a-lifetime marker that separated their past from their future forever. What a difference a choice makes!

Principle #3: The Focus

An initial decision to follow is admirable but does not ensure a person will continue to follow. For example, if a person says, "I'm going to follow the car in front of me," but then looks down and reads the newspaper for a few minutes while the other car drives away, that person is going to have a tough time following. What is lacking? Focus—the basic discipline of following. A decision to follow requires sustained focus on the leader.

The Israelites experienced this in the desert as God led them with the pillars of cloud and fire. God became the focus of their lives, the force that influenced every decision. Their focus made them hypersensitive to God's activity.

To follow without the ongoing discipline of focusing on the leader is silly, like a student who states her intention of being valedictorian but then never attends class. The goal is admirable but is impossible if the required discipline is lacking.

Principle #4: The Adjustment

Focusing on the leader is admirable, but it, too, is inadequate if it does not result in a decision to move in new directions in response to the changing activity of the leader. Following requires a submissive attitude, a willingness to adjust continually to the leader's initiative. Nothing tests the resolve of the follower more than this step in the process. There are times when the follower may observe the leader changing directions and say, "I don't want to go there." And so he stays where he is while the leader drives away. Immediately, the roles change; the process stops. The follower who chooses not to follow is no longer a follower.

This occurred with the Israelites. God led them to the edge of the promised land and commanded them to occupy it. They took a peek, completed a situation analysis, and said, "No thanks." So God let them wander in circles for forty years while they pondered their decision. He continued to remind them of His presence through the pillar of cloud and fire, but their attitudes never changed; as a result, the adults died in the desert—a grim reminder of the high price of a stubborn heart.

Principle #5: The Relationship

As a person becomes aware of a need, chooses to follow a leader, focuses on the leader, then responds over time to what the leader does, a relationship develops. By nature, following is relational. Rather than simply making a trip, the follower can know the leader on a deeper level. The follower can learn what the leader does, how he travels, where he goes, and what he prefers. The follower, in time, can discern "the ways" of the leader.

God's goal for the Israelites was not simply to get them from Egypt to the promised land. He wanted them to develop an intimate relationship with Him. He wanted them to be His people, and He wanted them to love Him as their God. The journey through the wilderness gave the Israelites the opportunity to develop a unique relationship with Him. Unfortunately, the people turned their backs on God and missed the relationship He offered.

Principle #6: The Change

The process of following and the relationship between a leader and a follower inevitably changes the follower. The change is not automatic, but it is profound. In fact, following a leader for an extended period of time is a proven method of transformation. The initial decision to follow, coupled with the focus, the adjustments, and the relationship that develops, profoundly influences the follower and brings about significant changes. Rather than a temporary adjustment in behavior, a "following" relationship creates a slow transformational process that results in lasting change.

The change, unfortunately, is not always for good—as illustrated in the Israelites. Although they went through the "following" process, they refused to adjust their lives as God required. They became stiff-necked and stubborn, ultimately rejecting their relationship with God. In the end, the adults of the exodus generation died without ever reaching the promised land. Only their children experienced the full cycle of the following process and ultimately received all the benefits of change. The children of the exodus were transformed in time from slaves to spiritual warriors, from desert whiners to men and women willing to fight in faith for the land God had promised them. Their lives contrasted sharply with those of their parents, who resisted God's change process and ultimately died as slaves to their own stubbornness.

Principle #7: The Destination

Although a close relationship with the leader and transformation in the follower's life are strong incentives, the process of following includes an ultimate reward: the destination. The follower joins the leader because the follower believes the leader knows the way; the leader is going someplace the follower wants to go. Getting there is the final reward. Even though the other incentives have stand-alone value, they do not diminish the importance of the final destination.

Throughout the Israelites' experiences, God continually reminded them of their destination: the promised land. He described the end of the journey in symbolic terms since they could not envision it. As a result, He motivated them with the promise of a "land flowing with milk and honey" (Exod. 3:8). One day, the children of the exodus generation stood on the hill and looked down on that promised land.

At that point, they knew that the destination had been worth the journey; they knew the land was everything God had promised.

FOLLOWING UP THE FOLLOWING TEST

How about trying that first Followology test question again? You remember the one about Car A and Car B? Well . . . maybe not. But at least you're ready if anyone asks to describe the seven principles in the process of following. Following always begins with an awareness of need. Without need there is no motivation to follow the leader. Following the leader begins with an initial choice—there is a time when you choose to follow or you choose to stay where you are. You are free to choose, but you are responsible for your choice. If you choose to follow, you must focus on the leader. Focus must become your central discipline as a follower. If the leader is not the central focus of your life, you'll get lost. If you are focusing on the leader, you'll have a continual string of choices to make as you decide if you will continue to go where the leader goes. Without a submissive attitude, you will not adjust your life to the changing requirements of the leader. If, however, you make the adjustments and stay with the leader, you will know the leader on increasingly deeper levels. That relationship, in time, will change you. Then at some point, you will reach your destination. In the end, your relationship with the leader, the changes in your life, and the destination you reach will be your rewards for following.

When you follow, you are going where the leader goes. Yet that simple process will change your life. How important is following? Why not ask the greatest followologist? You may be surprised (and encouraged) by the answer as we begin part 2 in our quest to become world-class followers of Jesus.

II

BUILDING A FOUNDATION
FOR FOLLOWING JESUS

Followism 4:   Following is important.
Followism 5:   If you don't know the way,
                you should follow the leader.
       ▶ Principle #1: The Need

Followism 6:   Following begins with an initial choice.
       ▶ Principle #2: The Choice

Followism 7:   Following requires focus.
       ▶ Principle #3: The Focus

Followism 8:   Following requires continual adjustment
                to the leader.
       ▶ Principle #4: The Adjustment

Followism 9:   Following builds relationship.
       ▶ Principle #5: The Relationship

Followism 10:   Following changes followers.
       ▶ Principle #6: The Change

Followism 11:   Followers go where their leaders are going.
       ▶ Principle #7: The Destination

JESUS, THE GREAT FOLLOWOLOGIST

4

Following is important.

How do you determine what is important to someone? One way is to look and listen for an extended period of time. If you hear the person talking about a particular topic repeatedly for years, you can assume it is more than an ideological hobbyhorse; rather, it is something about which the person cares deeply. In the same way, if you observe the person making decisions and ordering his daily life based on the topic you've heard him discussing, you can be sure you have unlocked an important key to that individual's value system. Words plus actions equal core life principles. Find these and you have discovered the forces that motivate another person. You now possess vital information that can help you understand that person on a deeper level.

Let's apply this process to Jesus. What did He talk about repeatedly during His earthly ministry? What concept affected the way He lived His life and the way He related to people? By now, you can guess that one of the defining themes in Jesus' life was "following."

Jesus was a followologist. Certainly, He did not refer to Himself as a followologist, but what better description for a person who talked about following as much as He did? Although most of us recall that Jesus began His ministry by inviting people to follow Him, I was surprised to discover that "following" remained a central focus for Jesus throughout His ministry. Consider a few selected passages that illustrate the priority Jesus placed on following as the central process of discipleship.

BIBLICAL EXAMPLES OF FOLLOWING

From the Beginning

When Jesus launched His earthly ministry, He invited people to follow Him. As He passed fishermen, tax collectors, and others, He challenged them to leave their old lives behind and fall in line behind Him.

> The next day Jesus decided to leave for Galilee. Finding Philip, he said to him, "Follow me." (John 1:43)
>
> "Come, follow me," Jesus said, "and I will make you fishers of men." (Matt. 4:19)
>
> As Jesus went on from there, he saw a man named Matthew sitting at the tax collector's booth. "Follow me," [Jesus] told him, and Matthew got up and followed him. (Matt. 9:9)

Counting the Cost

As Jesus performed miracles and His popularity inevitably swelled, Jesus challenged the crowds to stop following Him because of selfish interests but to commit their lives to Him in full discipleship. "Then he called the crowd to him along with his disciples and said: 'If anyone would come after me, he must deny himself and take up his cross and follow me'" (Mark 8:34).

His challenge to commitment produced discipleship "wannabes." So Jesus tested their desire to follow Him by probing their understanding of the price they would have to pay if they came with Him.

> As they were walking along the road, a man said to him, "I will follow you wherever you go." Jesus replied, "Foxes have holes and birds of the air have nests, but the Son of Man has no place to lay his head." He said to another man, "Follow me." But the man replied, "Lord, first let me go and bury my father." Jesus said to him, "Let the dead bury their own dead, but you go and proclaim the kingdom of God." Still another said, "I will follow you, Lord; but first let me go back and say good-by to my family." Jesus replied, "No one who puts his hand to the plow and looks back is fit for service in the kingdom of God." (Luke 9:57–62)

When the Going Gets Tough

Toward the end of His earthly ministry, Jesus sought to prepare His disciples for what was to come. To do so, He encouraged them with the language of Followology. He told them more than they could understand but bolstered their faith for the impending challenge: "Simon Peter asked him, 'Lord, where are you going?' Jesus replied, 'Where I am going, you cannot follow now, but you will follow later.' Peter asked, 'Lord, why can't I follow you now? I will lay down my life for you'" (John 13:36–37).

In the darkest hours of His life, as Jesus prepared for the cross and then as He took the long walk up Calvary, people continued to follow Him: "Jesus went out as usual to the Mount of Olives, and his disciples followed him" (Luke 22:39). "A large number of people followed him, including women who mourned and wailed for him" (Luke 23:27).

The Last Word of Followology

After His crucifixion and resurrection, Jesus met again with His disciples. All had failed Him, especially Peter, who had denied Him three times. But Jesus offered forgiveness and hope and extended a new call to discipleship by evoking the same language He had used to extend the initial call to discipleship years before: "Then [Jesus] said to him, 'Follow me!' Peter turned and saw that the disciple whom Jesus loved was following them. . . . When Peter saw him, he asked, 'Lord, what about him?' Jesus answered, 'If I want him to remain alive until I return, what is that to you? You must follow me'" (John 21:19–20, 22).

An Invitation to Discipleship

Jesus' first invitation was for people to follow Him, and then throughout His ministry He continually challenged them to follow Him with full commitment. At the close of His ministry, He challenged His most committed disciples to follow Him through all that was to come, and ultimately He ended His ministry by extending fresh invitations to follow once again. Wouldn't you say that "following" was important to Jesus?

The process of following is profound and powerful. For that reason, Jesus made following a central dimension of His leadership and discipleship strategy. Time was short. At the most, He had three or four years to involve ordinary people in a change process that would revolutionize their lives and prepare them for the most significant leadership challenge in history. Pumping them full of information would not work because He needed more than human storage bins for spiritual facts. He wanted transformed people, infused with a new value system and joined heart to heart with Him in spirit and purpose. To accomplish these purposes, Jesus deployed a strategy that was elegantly simple: He invited people to follow Him—initially, continually, drawing them deeper and deeper into His life, helping them learn the way as they remained with Him.

In contrast to other strategies, the "following" strategy was inclusive. Anyone could follow—even spiritual novices, even those in the slow group. Jesus invited everyone He met, and those who responded discovered that following Jesus transformed their lives.

THE WISDOM OF THE PROCESS

How did the process of following Jesus transform them? What key elements held some people back while propelling others forward? Ah, the answers to those questions are yet to come in our study. For now, ponder this simple truth: God has always been a followologist, so following must be important.

God emphasized following in His relationship with the Israelites as He led them through the desert. We find other examples of God's emphasis on following throughout the Old Testament in the stories of the patriarchs, judges, kings, and prophets. As we turn the pages to the New Testament, we discover the ultimate story of followology in the Gospels—the story of Jesus, the greatest followologist.

Our goal is to become better followers of Jesus today. Here's the good news: Following Jesus is not limited to the first century. In fact, following Jesus—not just His teachings, but actually following Him— is the central discipline of Christianity today.

In the remainder of part 2, we're going to discover how Jesus used the seven principles in the following process to change the lives of His disciples. His goal with them was transformation, not information, so that should be our goal as well. Our quest is to discover how following Jesus radically changed the lives of twelve ordinary people. For if they could follow Jesus, so can we. If they could change, we can too.

It all begins with the first principle in the following process, the principle that unleashes our motivation to follow Jesus today.

Playing Follow the Leader

5

If you don't know the way,
you should follow the leader.

Step #1: The Need Principle

As the sun rose over a land-locked lake, four commercial fishermen worked in fatigued silence. Another night. Another meager catch. Now nets demanded repairs and boats required attention. A few hours of rest and then the relentless drill would begin again as it would each day until old age or illness ended the cycle. Then they would die and be forgotten. But for the moment, they refused to think about such things. They had work to do. And they must work before they could rest so that they could work again.

Away from the lake in the city's business district, a government worker prepared for another day of confrontations. The rules of success in his line of work were simple: for him to win, everyone he encountered had to lose. He knew the game when he started, so he played hard and used skills honed over the years—threats, coercion, manipulation. Whatever was required, he was prepared to do. That was his job—at least the part of the job that belonged to him. Of the money he collected, the government demanded a fixed amount and allowed him to keep the rest. It was a lucrative arrangement for those who were good at it. And he was very good at it. This was no job for soft-hearts who wanted to win friends and influence people. Every day the game was the same. Only the faces changed. Yes, he had done well. But he had paid a price—a very high price.

On the outskirts of town, a political activist, a zealot some would say, walked home from a clandestine meeting. It had been another night of impassioned speeches and grandiose plans, another meeting of the malcontents unwilling to wait for political change. While the masses waited and accommodated the occupiers, the activists developed plans and watched for the moment to deal the blow that would bring ultimate change. But would it be enough? he wondered. Could the anger that fueled their passion build a nation as well as destroy an enemy? He refused to dwell on such thoughts. The line had been drawn, and he had stepped over. No matter what the future held, he would not turn away.

In a small room, a young intellectual's mind continued to race. He had been unable to sleep after the lively exchange the night before. For hours, he had pondered the questions asked and the responses given. With relentless objectivity, he evaluated his contribution to the discussion and chided himself for his emotional outbursts. How could he think clearly when his emotions captured and carried him, causing him to utter bold declarations driven by passion rather than logic? He had to know the answers. He must understand. The future belonged to those with keen minds who could hold emotions at bay. Yet he wondered if his knowledge could change anything. His mind churned questions that evaded answers. The darkest questions leered at him, defying him to answer them. In the end, he wondered if anything he did had meaning. Did truth exist, or were there only questions?

In other places, people scattered throughout the city, doing what they did every day—nothing of distinction, nothing that set them apart from the crowd, nothing that made anyone remember their names. So they joined the commercial fishermen, the political activist, the government worker, and the intellectual in wistful longing that life could be more and different. But nothing offered promise that life could change. Nothing.

THEY-R-US

Who are those guys? They are Jesus' twelve disciples, the dozen ordinary men Michaelangelo helped us visualize through his painting *The Last Supper*. You know—the one where someone said, "All right; everyone on this side of the table." Those twelve men are us. Understand them and we can discover more about ourselves. Grasp what Jesus did in their lives and we can glimpse what Jesus wants to do in us. The Gospel writers provide names and snippets of information about each of the disciples who first followed Jesus.

Jesus went up on a mountainside and called to him those he wanted, and they came to him. He appointed twelve—designating them apostles—that they might be with him and that he might send them out to preach and to have authority to drive out demons. These are the twelve he appointed: Simon (to whom he gave the name Peter); James son of Zebedee and his brother John (to them he gave the name Boanerges, which means Sons of Thunder); Andrew, Philip, Bartholomew, Matthew, Thomas, James, son of Alphaeus, Thaddaeus, Simon the Zealot and Judas Iscariot, who betrayed him. (Mark 3:13–19)

Even with this list, it is still easy to get confused, so let's match the names with the descriptions at the beginning of this chapter. Start with the four commercial fishermen—Simon Peter and his brother, Andrew, and James and his brother, John. Then add Matthew, the tax collector—what we might call a government worker. Don't forget Simon, always referred to as a zealot—a first-century radical political activist. Most people remember Thomas, focusing on his doubts while overlooking his intellectual bent and his passion. No one can forget Judas, the betrayer. That leaves the final four who did nothing notorious or memorable that we know of from the biblical accounts—Philip, Bartholomew, James son of Alphaeus, and Thaddaeus.

So much for the names; let's get back to the question: who are those guys? Well, they were ordinary people who were minding their own business until one day when Jesus walked by and invited them to follow Him. They left everything and became His disciples.

All right. That answers the "who." But what about the "why"? Why did they follow Jesus? Funny thing about that question—the Bible doesn't answer it. All we know is that Jesus invited them to come with Him and they did.

We know that two of them, Andrew and John, were spiritual seekers, interested enough to become disciples of John the Baptist, who later pointed them to Jesus. We know that Andrew and John believed that Jesus was the long-awaited Messiah because that is what they told others. At some level, all of them were searching for something, attempting to scratch an itch they couldn't quite reach. So when Jesus walked by, following Him became the top priority in their lives.

We do not know the details behind each decision to follow Jesus. The fishermen, the tax collector, the intellectual, the political zealot, and the "good old boys" heard Jesus' invitation to discipleship and said, "Yes, I'll follow."

Each made a choice. A choice motivated by an awareness that something was missing in their lives. A choice activated by faith that Jesus was going where they wanted to go. A choice made with less-than-complete information, but one driven by faith's spiritual instincts. They followed Jesus because they didn't know the way. They believed Jesus knew the way. End of discussion.

It always works that way. The motivation to follow is always in direct proportion to one's awareness of the need to follow. When people believe they know the way or know what to do, they can become stubborn and ignore the leader. Unfortunately, I speak from painful (and in this case, expensive) personal experience.

DOWN THE LEADERSHIP DRIVEWAY

My father and I sat together in my car at the top of my sloped driveway. Twenty-five feet in front of us was the destination: the right side of my front-entry, divided, two-car garage. Sure, the driveway was steep. I pointed out, however, that my old Volvo was relatively small, and the garage door was relatively wide, which meant it should be relatively easy to slide through the opening with room to spare on either side. Plus, it was dangerous, I added, to leave the car parked out front, since the huge fir trees that surrounded my house occasionally chunked twenty-foot limbs at car windshields (something I had experienced the previous winter). So after carefully evaluating the risks and the rewards, I convinced myself that not only could we get into the garage as I proposed, we simply had no alternative. Boldly, I declared my intent.

Silence.

Then my father said, "Since you don't have the chains on, that ice may give you trouble. I don't think you can get into the garage."

That really ticked me off. Yes, a layer of ice covered the driveway, but several inches of snow covered the ice. The snow would create enough traction for us to ease down the driveway and into the garage. After two full days of messing with snow chains (putting them on for the residential streets and taking them off for the highway, then putting them back on for the residential streets once again), I wanted to park my car in the garage and stay home. Ignoring my father's warnings, I gave the car a drop of gas and eased over the crest of the hill in complete control of the situation. Confidently, I clutched the steering wheel. My father reached out to brace himself against the dash with one hand—an ominous prophecy of what was to come.

For the first few feet, we rolled straight toward the open right-side garage door. Momentarily, confidence welled within me. Then, without warning, an unseen law of icy-driveway physics took control of the vehicle. Although I held the steering wheel perfectly straight, the car began to slide to the left, picking up speed as we moved down the driveway. My father braced himself with both hands.

Boom! The car rammed into the center wall section that separated the right side of my divided garage from the left. Crack! The house shook from the impact of the surprise attack. Wood split, and metal supporting frames buckled.

Instinctively, I shifted the car in reverse, but the wheels spun, and nothing happened. Then the grim reality dawned on me: my car would remain wedged in the front of my house like a driveway torpedo until the ice melted. Curious passersby saw my car and called the situation to my attention just in case I had missed it.

"See you had some trouble with your car," they said helpfully. "Yes," I responded. "I told my father we couldn't make it into the garage since the driveway was icy. But he insisted that we try."

A QUESTION OF MOTIVATION

One of the foundational followisms is, "If you don't know the way, you should follow the leader." I could have avoided a garage repair bill (not to mention great humiliation) had I heeded that principle. Yet, atop my driveway with ego on the line and a short distance to travel, my motivation to follow fell, and I moved ahead on my own. Bad decision. I thought I knew what to do. I felt self-sufficient, confident, and cocky. As a result, I crashed my house.

Lots of people today miscalculate their ability to control their lives. They feel self-sufficient, confident, and cocky. As a result they crash their lives. Jesus told us the truth in John 15:5 when He said,

"Apart from me you can do nothing." That spells out the situation in block letters. We don't know the way. We need a leader.

Who were those first followers of Jesus? People just like us who sensed that they didn't know the way. So when Jesus invited them to follow, they jumped at the opportunity. Motivation was no problem because they assessed their situation accurately.

Self-sufficiency is a lie. At the deepest level, none of us knows the way. But someone does. And the one who knows the way invites us to follow Him. So much for the "Need Principle" in Followology. Now the ball is in our court. It's decision time!

READY, SET, CHOOSE

*Following begins with
an initial choice.*

Step #2: The Choice Principle

Nothing tops dodgeball for separating the men from the boys. In dodgeball history, nothing tops the day Coach Bergin made his shocking announcement.

It was springtime. I was in seventh grade, and we had endured almost a full year of Coach Bergin. For eight months, he had tried to transform our group of nonathletes into hardened physical specimens. Under his relentless stare and shrill whistle, we had run until we threw up; done calisthenics until we ached; played sports in driving rain, biting cold, and sweltering heat; and endured the stench of the boys' locker room while listening to pep talks about the benefits of good health. Many of us dreamed about what we'd like to do to Coach Bergin if we ever had the chance. Suddenly, we did.

Coach Bergin lined the red, hard-rubber, cantaloupe-sized balls along the center line in the gym, then turned to us. "I'm going to play today," he stated matter-of-factly. "I'll lead this side; Ebert, you lead the other side." As he spoke, Eddie Ebert jumped up and ran onto the gym floor, giddy with excitement. Eddie was bigger than the rest of us, possibly because this was his third shot at seventh grade. But what Eddie lacked in academic prowess, he compensated for in dodgeball skills. Eddie was the best. No one wanted to get hit by a dodgeball Eddie hurled.

Coach Bergin continued. "All right. Choose your side and let's get started." With that, he walked to his half of the gym.

What an opportunity. What a dilemma. In a split second, every one of us had to decide if we would follow Coach Bergin or if we would follow Eddie. One choice promised security and safety. One choice held the enticing possibility of revenge.

The next few minutes revealed that our band of boys divided almost equally between those driven by security and those lured by revenge. I chose revenge.

The game began, and the wisdom of each choice became quickly apparent. Although we had watched Coach Bergin for a full year, we had never actually seen him do anything athletic. Whether he had other skills, we never learned. But one thing became painfully clear: Coach Bergin could throw a dodgeball.

With deadly accuracy, he began to pick off boys on my side. With uncanny ease, he rocketed ball after ball at my teammates. Unlike many of us who heaved our balls savagely but wildly, Coach Bergin fired balls like heat-seeking missiles. Splats, pops, and cries of pain filled the air. Still my team fought for our noble cause. We picked off our spineless classmates. A few brave souls even flung a ball or two at Coach Bergin. But he either deflected their shots or scooted out of the way untouched. Finally, my moment came.

With a ball hidden behind my back, I waited until Coach Bergin walked to the center stripe and fired two balls at my teammates in the far, back corner. While he was looking at his latest victims, I ran toward center court and zinged my ball at him with startling intensity. Visions of victory filled my mind. I would become a school legend—the kid who got Coach Bergin out during dodgeball.

At the last second, he saw me, turned, held out his right hand, and caught my red rubber missile with one hand. *Impossible*, I thought, but true. And although at that point I was technically out since he had caught my ball, Coach Bergin fired my ball at me, connecting with a deafening smack as I dove for the back of the gym.

With a red welt on my back and humiliation in my heart, I slithered to the sidelines to join my wounded comrades. The remaining moments of the game were not pretty. In the end, Coach Bergin and his minions won, and we, the gallant opposing team, were obliterated —including Eddie Ebert. We had chosen the leader we would follow. We made the wrong choice.

THE CHOICES THE DISCIPLES MADE

In Followology, the process always unfolds the same way. The Need Principle describes the motivation for following. Then the Choice

Principle focuses on the responsibility for following. If need convinces us we do not know the way, a choice must be made, a choice for which we will be held responsible.

A defining moment occurs. Before the choice, you are not following; after the choice, you are following.

In the previous chapter, we focused on the twelve men who became Jesus' core disciples. Jesus invited them to follow Him, and they said yes. It is fascinating to discover, however, that they did not make a full commitment to follow Jesus initially. In fact, it appears that at least some of the disciples followed Jesus on a less-than-full-time basis before He designated them as apostles.

The excellent harmony of the Gospels titled *The Greatest Story* by Cheney and Ellisen[1] helped me grasp this chronology for the first time. Although scholars debate the finer details of how to consolidate all the events recorded in Matthew, Mark, Luke, and John, I appreciate the timeline included in *The Greatest Story* because the authors included every element from all four Gospels then wove the accounts together in a single, readable story.

As I read the narrative with the perspective of a followologist, some fascinating insights popped out that I had missed in years of reading the Gospels separately. For example, I learned that Andrew and John were really the first followers of Jesus. Because they had identified with John the Baptist, they were with him the day he saw Jesus and said, "Look, the Lamb of God!" (John 1:36). Based on this startling statement, Andrew and John began to follow Jesus. After spending a day with Him, they were convinced He was the "real thing." So Andrew found his brother, Simon, and said, "We have found the Messiah" and then brought Simon to Jesus. The next day, Jesus personally invited Philip to follow Him, and Philip told his friend Nathanael, "We have found the one Moses wrote about in the Law, and about whom the prophets also wrote—Jesus of Nazareth, the son of Joseph" (John 1:45).

Apparently Nathanael, who did not become one of the twelve apostles, joined the other three men as Jesus' first disciples. They then followed Jesus to Cana in Galilee and marveled as Jesus changed water into wine. Later, they followed Jesus to Jerusalem and watched Him drive the money changers and sacrifice-sellers from the temple. They overheard Jesus describe spiritual birth to a leader of the Pharisees

named Nicodemus and were aghast as Jesus offered "living water" to a
Samaritan woman and then to a town full of Samaritans. On the way
back to Galilee, they witnessed Jesus' second miracle as He healed the
son of a royal official in Capernaum without ever seeing the boy.
Finally, they watched Jesus walk through a furious mob from His home-
town that wanted to throw Him off a cliff because He had offended
them with His teaching.

Although Jesus' first followers are not prominent in these
accounts, "disciples" are mentioned. We can assume Andrew, John,
Simon, and Philip were there, but they are not named. What is clear is
that a small group of people called "disciples" were with Jesus, observ-
ing Him, evaluating, seeking to reinforce their growing conviction that
He was the Messiah. This background makes the accounts in Matthew,
Mark, and Luke about Jesus' next invitation to discipleship even more
fascinating.

As Jesus completed His period of preparation, He began to preach
in the region of Galilee. There, by the sea, Jesus extended His memorable invitation to the four commercial fishermen (Andrew, Simon,
James, and John). "Come, follow me," Jesus said, "and I will make you
fishers of men" (Mark 1:18).

Decision time had come. The fishermen had to choose, and they
did. "At once they left their nets and followed him" (Mark 1:18). Luke
even adds another scene and tells of a morning when Jesus instructed
the four fishermen to return to the sea and try one more time for a
catch. Simon resisted since they had worked all night without results.
But he obeyed, and when their enormous catch began to break their
nets, Simon was overwhelmed and later fell at Jesus' knees and said,
"Go away from me, Lord; I am a sinful man!" (Luke 5:8). Luke tells us
that Simon and the others were astonished at the catch of fish. It was
then that Luke records: "So they pulled their boats up on shore, left
everything and followed him" (Luke 5:11).

Some time later, Jesus returned to Capernaum where He taught
and healed. News about Him began to spread and reached a tax collector named Matthew. Possibly no one was more surprised than he
was when Jesus walked by his collection booth and said, "Follow me."
But Matthew made the choice. He left his lucrative vocation and
joined Jesus. He rejoiced in his choice and immediately invited all his
friends to a party so he could introduce them to his new leader.

Matthew wanted his friends to make the choice to follow Jesus also (see Mark 2:13–17).

After that, Jesus spent a full night in prayer and then called together all His followers on a mountainside and announced the names of the twelve who would have special access to Him as apostles.

When Jesus called out the names Simon, Andrew, James, John, and Matthew, He affirmed the choice they began making months before when He invited them to follow. Perhaps the others Jesus named that day had followed Him along with these five; we don't know. But we sense their choice was deliberate, not impulsive.

I recognize that some scholars believe that the various accounts from the four Gospels reflect personal perspectives on the same stories. For this reason, they may disagree with the chronology on which I've based these observations. Yet, as a followologist and a student of human nature, it is easier for me to believe that Jesus' first followers struggled with their commitment to follow Him in the same way most of us do. Yes, there was an initial decision to follow; but the decision came after people determined that Jesus was the leader who knew the way. His teaching, His miracles, and His lifestyle convinced them. So at the crucial moment, they made their choice, left everything, and followed Jesus. Years later when the crowds deserted Him, Jesus asked the twelve if they were going to leave also. Simon Peter answered without hesitation: "Lord, to whom shall we go? You have the words of eternal life. We believe and know that you are the Holy One of God" (John 6:68–69).

Following always begins with an initial choice. It is the choice that changes everything—for the one making the choice and for others. History affirms the truth of this statement, sometimes with gleaming monuments to right choices but also with tragic monuments to wrong choices.

The High Price of a Wrong Choice

The names sound ordinary: Martin, Alfred, Arthur, Julius, Karl, and others. But on October 1, 1946, judges read verdicts that sealed their fate and revealed the folly of their choice to follow the wrong leader.

On November 20, 1945, the Nuremberg International Military Tribunal began a trial that lasted for ten months. Those charged with crimes against humanity did not look like leaders of a great nation. Instead, those who watched said they looked like ordinary people picked off the street. Gone was the chin-jutting arrogance that once exuded in Nazi newsreels.

The world held these Nazi leaders accountable for their part in the murder of six million Jews, the torture of prisoners of war, the enslavement of the citizens of occupied nations, as well as sadistic medical experiments. Notably absent was their leader, Adolph Hitler, who missed his day in court by killing himself as the war ended. But his followers did not escape judgment on October 16, 1946. That day, the following men were executed by hanging:

> Joachim von Ribbentrop, Hitler's foreign minister.
> Hans Frank, administrator of occupied Poland.
> Wilhelm Frick, Hitler's first interior minister.
> Ernst Kaltenbrunner, head of Reich Main Security office, which administered the death and concentration camps.
> Alfred Rosenberg, Nazi Party ideologist.
> Fritz Sauchkel, overseer of slave labor program.
> Julius Steicher, Hitler's propaganda chief and editor of the anti-Semitic newspaper, *Der Stuermer.*
> Wilhelm Keitel, chief of military high command.
> Arthur Seyss-Inquart, Reich commissioner for occupied Netherlands.
> Only Hermann Goering, Hitler's hand-picked successor and head of the German air force, escaped judgment on October 16. He killed himself with a poison capsule in his cell the day before.

In all, twenty-one of Hitler's top leaders were tried. All twenty-one pleaded innocent but were ultimately convicted. In time, nearly two hundred more Nazi leaders were tried in twelve successive international military trials at Nuremberg. Thousands more were tried by national courts in West and East Germany and in the Soviet Union, Poland, Czechoslovakia, and countries invaded by Hitler's legions. The world paid a high price for Hitler's folly, but in the end, Hitler and his followers paid as well. The price is always high when people follow the wrong leader.[2]

Responsible for Our Choice

No one said that choosing the leader to whom we will commit our lives is easy. It was not easy for Jesus' first followers; it is not easy for us. However, the knowledge of what is at stake in that choice sobers us with the responsibility for that choice. Certainly, our personal stake in eternity hinges on the decision we make. But our choice will influence others. If we choose to follow Jesus, we set in motion a spiritual chain reaction of blessing. Hitler's men made a choice that triggered a chain reaction of unimaginable evil.

What a difference a choice makes. I have decided to follow Jesus. No turning back. No turning back. What about you?

7

PAY ATTENTION

Following requires focus.

Step #3: The Focus Principle

"Come on. This isn't brain surgery!" Perhaps you've heard people say that when they encounter a problem that is challenging but not impossible. But have you ever wondered what brain surgeons say? In the middle of an operation, they can't say, "Come on. This isn't brain surgery." It's an intriguing problem.

Frankly, I had not thought about it until I heard a segment on *All Things Considered*, a program on National Public Radio. The reporting staff posed the question, then began a quest for the answer.

First, they called a brain surgeon and asked what he and other brain surgeons say when they encounter challenging but not impossible problems. He suggested that the appropriate response among brain surgeons might be, "Come on. This isn't rocket science!"

Ah, but that answer raised another question. What do rocket scientists say in a similar situation? So the NPR staff asked a rocket scientist. He thought his colleagues might say, "Come on. This isn't theoretical physics!"

Oops—another question. You guessed it. The staff talked with a theoretical physicist (and I suspect those folks are tough to find). When asked the same question, his response was somewhat vague. Apparently, no consensus exists among theoretical physicists for an appropriate statement when confronted with a problem that is challenging but not impossible.

So what do you suggest they say? How about, "This isn't Followology." Wrong. Followology, once understood, is simple. The theoretical physicists will have to decide on a snappy response at their next convention—and they can't use Followology!

The truth is that anything familiar seems simpler than something unfamiliar. Any process analyzed and organized is easier to grasp than one that remains tangled in complexity. The same is true with Followology. Because you are learning the seven principles in the following process, you can now see spiritual implications for discipleship that others miss. Focus in Followology is not difficult to grasp. It's not brain surgery, rocket science, or theoretical physics, but the discipline of paying attention spiritually is essential if we want to become better followers of Jesus. Fortunately, the Bible provides numerous passages that address this issue. However, we find these truths in unusual places.

THE IMPORTANCE OF TRAVELING HERE TO THERE

Have you ever noticed how many times the Gospels mention Jesus moving from one place to another? If you like to underline verses in your Bible, I suspect you have not underlined many passages about Jesus traveling from Point A to Point B. Frankly, in the past, I thought these verses were boring (true, but boring). If the text said that Jesus' disciples were with Him in Place A and that they were still with Him in Place B, I believe it happened just that way. All the same, those passages reminded me of reading the flight information monitor in the airport—informative but not riveting.

My perspective changed, however, when I became a followologist. Suddenly, those Place A to Place B passages intrigued me. Rather than simply skimming, I researched them, seeking to understand geography, topography, and distances. Before I explain why, let's work on three short cases about Jesus and His disciples from the Gospel of John.

One word of warning: if you find your mind overheating at any point during these studies, stop thinking immediately. Relax for a few moments and allow your mind to cool down before continuing. Followology is a new field, and we cannot afford to lose even one budding followologist!

Case Study #1: From Bethany to Cana

Jesus was in Bethany, a town close to Jerusalem in the southern part of the country. He encountered several men (Andrew, Simon Peter, Philip, and Nathanael were mentioned) and challenged them to follow

Him. Jesus then decided to leave for Galilee in the northern part of the country where He attended a wedding in a city named Cana. In John 2, we learn that Jesus' disciples attended the wedding with Him. Question: How did Jesus' disciples get from Bethany to Cana?

Case Study #2: From Capernaum to Jerusalem

When it was almost time for the Jewish Passover, Jesus left Capernaum (in Galilee) and traveled south again to Judea, up the mountain to the city of Jerusalem. Once there, He went to the temple and drove out the salesmen and money changers. In John 3, we find that Jesus' disciples were still with Him. Question: How did Jesus' disciples get from Capernaum to Jerusalem?

Case Study #3: A Trip through Samaria

After a clandestine meeting with a Jewish leader named Nicodemus and increased attention by the Pharisees, Jesus left Judea and traveled north again to Galilee. Rather than avoiding the area in between called Samaria, Jesus traveled directly through it and stopped at a city named Sychar. In John 4, we discover that Jesus' disciples were still with Him. Question: How did the disciples get from Judea to Samaria?

NOT THEORETICAL FOLLOWOLOGY

Our three case studies raise three micro-questions that combine to form one macro-question. Let's review the micro-questions:

> How did Jesus' disciples get from Bethany to Cana?
> How did Jesus' disciples get from Capernaum to Jerusalem?
> How did Jesus' disciples travel through Samaria?

Of course, the macro-question is how did Jesus' disciples get from "Point A" to "Point B"?

After exhaustive research on this subject, I'm prepared to go out on a limb with an answer. All indicators suggest that they followed Jesus.

Now, stay with me on this one. If this is correct, this means that these crack disciples must have paid close attention to Jesus and noticed when He started walking down the road. Or, perhaps Jesus turned to them and said, "I'm heading up to Cana now. You can come if you want to." We do not know exactly what they did, but in some way the disciples monitored Jesus' activity sufficiently enough to notice when He left town. That's what we mean by "focus." They paid attention to what Jesus was doing. Because they focused, they could follow. Whew! That was tough, but we made it through.

Back to Physical Following

Since Followology is an experiential science, let's switch to a physical example. Imagine you are in a caravan of cars traveling to a destination unknown to you. Without a map or written directions, your only hope is to follow the car in front of you, a car driven by the one person in your group who knows the way.

You know that you do not know the way, so you are highly motivated to follow the leader. You believe the person in the first car is going where you want to go and knows the way, so you have made the choice to follow. You recognize that you cannot follow the leader if you do not focus on the leader. Motivation and commitment are at peak levels. But as you wait at a red light, you glance down to change the station on your radio. You fumble with the tuner, fiddle with the seek and scan buttons, and finally find the perfect station. Suddenly, the car behind you blasts a full-power honk. You look up, startled. The light is green. There are no cars in front of you. The car you intended to follow is nowhere in sight. You look straight ahead, to the right, to the left. Nothing. The lead car has vanished and with it any hope you had of reaching your destination.

A far-fetched situation? Of course not. All of us have been there, committed to following but placed in crisis mode because we failed to focus on the leader. One moment we were following the leader; seconds later, we were totally lost—victims of a loss of focus.

It happens the same way spiritually. In spite of our best intentions to focus on our relationship with God and to allow the Holy Spirit to work in our lives, we become distracted. In part 3 we will address one of the most important topics of Followology: following a leader you cannot see. But for now, it is important to think about following in its purest form, following Jesus as the first disciples did. Even in their unique situation, following was not automatic. Even though they had the privilege of knowing Jesus as a flesh-and-blood man, they still had to develop the discipline of focus so they could follow Him.

The simple followism "Following begins with focus" captures a truth that can transform our spiritual lives. Certainly, we struggle today to focus on Jesus, to see what He is doing and where He is going. Following Jesus is difficult, but do we desperately want to see Jesus? Are we paying attention spiritually as if our lives depended on it? Are we fully convicted of our continual need to look for Him, to focus on Him, to see Him? Until we become highly motivated to see Jesus we will never pay the price required to discipline our lives so we can see Him.

Remember the pillars of cloud and fire that God used to lead the Israelites through the wilderness? God took the initiative, but the people still had to pay attention. We don't have a pillar to follow as they did. We don't have Jesus in the flesh to follow as the first disciples did. But we can get ahead by staying behind, if focusing on Jesus becomes the highest priority in our lives.

If you had awakened an Israelite in the wilderness from a dead sleep, what is the first thing he might have said? "Where's the pillar?"

If you had awakened one of the first disciples from a dead sleep, what is the first thing he might have said? "Where's Jesus?"

If someone wakes you up from a dead sleep, what is the first thing you should say?

You can't follow if you don't focus. God is not hiding from us. Remember His promise: "You will seek me and find me when you seek me with all your heart" (Jer. 29:13). We'll learn more about the "how" later. For now, concentrate on the "what." FOCUS!

FOLLOWING UNCONDITIONALLY

Following requires continual adjustment to the leader.

8

Step #4: The Adjustment Principle

Leaders lead; followers follow. Leaders set the pace; followers adjust. Sometimes keeping up with the leader becomes a big challenge. That's what happened in day three of our great Texas-to-Oregon Trail road trip I told you about earlier. Two old cars. Three valiant drivers—me, Dean, and my father, "Big Bill."

Our two-car caravan headed northwest out of the Mojave Desert through the winding hills on the state highway. Leaving the freeway was a bold, calculated move by Big Bill to save time. Distance-wise, he was right. Time-wise, he miscalculated. The winding, two-lane road was choked with cars and tour buses. Rather than the relative ease of freeway travel, driving became tense hours of quick-dart passing punctuated with waiting, frustration, and exhaust fumes.

According to the predetermined pattern of driver rotation, I led the way in Whitie (our old Volvo) with Big Bill handling convoy communications over the CB radio from the "shotgun" position. Dean followed in the Blue Goose (our ancient Oldsmobile).

As it became clear Big Bill had made an uncharacteristically poor decision in his choice of routes, he began a counter-offensive: plotting map coordinates, calculating distances, and offering frequent instructions to me and Dean about passing opportunities.

My dad has many endearing qualities; however, when he slips into his General Patton role, things get tense for the foot soldiers. As the hours passed, it was no picnic for me in command post Whitie, and I sensed growing frustration with Dean in the Blue Goose.

After guiding us masterfully past a long series of tour buses and slow moving cars for several hours, Big Bill began to relax. The battle

41

had been tough but we had made up lost time. Just then, Dean's voice cracked over the CB. "Break for Whitie. You got the Blue Goose here. I'm going to pull over for a minute."

Sensing a Code Red emergency, Big Bill returned to full alert. Grabbing the CB, he responded, "Come back, Blue Goose. Are you having car trouble?" Crack. Pop. Static. "Big negatorie," Dean responded. "We're experiencing driver trouble of a personal nature, and we're going to pull over for a pit stop. Over."

Instantly, Big Bill assessed the potential impact. In the time required for the proposed stop, two hours' worth of slow-moving cars and tour buses would pass us, and the challenge of passing them would begin again. The proposed stop for the Blue Goose was operationally unthinkable.

"Break for the Blue Goose," Big Bill said. "We're almost out of the hills. Can you wait?" he asked, in a tone that supplied the intended answer.

The radio was silent for a moment, then it cracked to life. "Negatorie," Dean responded. "We've got a personal problem of a significant nature back here. I've *got* to pull over."

As road fate would have it, we entered a stretch of highway blasted out of rock that left narrow shoulders along the road with no visual protection. After driving several more miles, Big Bill returned to the airwaves with a status report. "I think we're coming to a good spot; get ready to pull off."

"You got the Blue Goose here," responded Dean's familiar voice. "No need to stop. I took care of the problem."

Big Bill looked at me and then picked up the microphone. "You want to tell us how you took care of this problem, Blue Goose?" After a moment's pause, the radio cracked once again. "I bit the top off a Coke can," Dean responded. "Blue Goose out."

Dean never provided details about his Coke can solution. We didn't ask. Sometimes it's best if you don't know the details. Over the years, though, I have reflected on Dean's situation, imagining the tactical challenge he faced and contemplating the potential risks he endured. I know that Dean moved up several spots on Big Bill's road warrior ranking. The topless, teeth-marked Coke can became an honorable symbol of the adjustments one must make to stay with the leader.

The Adjustment Principle describes the fourth step in the following process. Followers who are motivated to follow a leader assume responsibility for choosing their leader and develop the discipline of focusing on their leader must then nurture an attitude of submission to that leader. Since the leader determines the agenda and sets the pace, the follower must adjust.

CONDITIONAL ADJUSTMENTS

Lots of people are willing to follow—if they can specify the terms. Lots of people will follow—if the leader will adjust to their needs. Nothing inappropriate or unreasonable; just a few simple accommodations are all that is needed. Yet "conditions" always indicate a battle for control. Who will lead? Who will follow? Who is in charge? Who will adjust?

During His earthly ministry, Jesus invited large numbers of people to follow Him. Their responses help us understand the challenge of developing an attitude of unconditional spiritual submission to Jesus' leadership in our lives today

Unspoken Conditions

One day, a teacher of the law expressed his desire to follow Jesus. On the surface, he sounded like a follower with the perfect attitude: "Then a teacher of the law came to him and said, 'Teacher, I will follow you wherever you go.' Jesus replied, 'Foxes have holes and birds of the air have nests, but the Son of Man has no place to lay his head'" (Matt. 8:19–20).

Jesus discerned unspoken conditions in this man's heart. The teacher said he was willing to follow Jesus without reservation. In reality, his concept of discipleship presupposed that a minimum level of personal needs would be met along the way. As Jesus described the demands of discipleship, the teacher's secret expectations were revealed. Apparently, he did not mean "anywhere" when he said he would follow Jesus. That "anywhere" was just a figure of speech. He was willing to follow Jesus anywhere as long as the destination was reasonable and the accommodations were appropriate.

Many today are like that teacher. In an emotional moment, they step up and declare their desire to follow Jesus no matter where He leads and no matter what it costs. Unfortunately, such sincere intentions are often untested by physical or spiritual realities. So when the unemotional, long, faithful walk behind Jesus begins, the followers fade. They are not bad people, simply spiritually naive. That's why Jesus promised no fantasy trip with fish fries and water walks. Jesus knew the road ahead would be hard, and He could not take an easier route to accommodate the expectations of the ill-prepared.

A spiritual crisis exists today because too many religious leaders have played on people's spiritual naiveté by marketing Christianity as a religious Disneyland filled with miracle rides, money trees, and happiness machines. Initially people snap up the tickets but later discover the scam. When they do, expectations plummet and disillusionment rules. What a contrast with Jesus. He simply told people the truth up front. Discipleship is tough but worth it.

Commitment with Stings Attached

Another group expressed their desire to follow Jesus. Unlike the teacher with unspoken expectations, these people were forthright about the adjustments Jesus would need to make before they would follow Him. "Another disciple said to him, 'Lord, first let me go and bury my father.' But Jesus told him, 'Follow me, and let the dead bury their own dead'" (Matt. 8:21–22).

Although Jesus' response sounded harsh, He discerned that this man's family commitments provided an excuse to discipleship. Under this guise, the man could express his desire to follow Jesus without ever doing so. Jesus would have none of it. Another potential follower added a second verse to the "family first" chorus: "I will follow you, Lord; but first let me go back and say good-bye to my family" (Luke 9:61).

Another reasonable request. But Jesus knew this man could only go forward if he never looked back. The lure of family and comfort would be too great for him. If he went back, he would never follow. So Jesus issued this challenge: "Jesus replied, 'No one who puts his hand to the plow and looks back is fit for service in the kingdom of God'" (Luke 9:62).

As far as we know, neither of these men ever followed Jesus. He rejected their conditions, and they were unwilling to adjust their lives. On the surface, their requests sounded reasonable. Both fell in the category of "making family a priority." Surely Jesus could support that. In these cases, however, the requests indicated spiritual heart problems. These people were willing to follow Jesus only on their terms. They were unwilling to submit unconditionally to Jesus as their leader. Instead, they stated their terms and expected Him to comply; they offered the deal and expected Jesus to meet their demands.

Most of us can identify with these people. How easy it is to say, "I'll follow Jesus after my career is on track." Or, "I'll follow Jesus after my children are through college." Or, "I'll follow Jesus after we face this health crisis." The truth is, there will always be good reasons to follow Jesus with full devotion later. Yet we have no right to negotiate the terms under which we will be disciples. Jesus is the leader. He sets the terms. We, as the followers, must make the adjustments.

Excuses Disguised as Conditions

Jesus helps us understand a final group of followers in His parable about the man who invited guests to a great banquet. Jesus implied that all who received the invitation had a relationship with the host and were expected to attend. In every case, however, they declined. "But they all alike began to make excuses. The first said, 'I have just bought a field, and I must go and see it. Please excuse me.' Another said, 'I have just bought five yoke of oxen, and I'm on my way to try them out. Please excuse me.' Still another said, 'I just got married, so I can't come'" (Luke 14:18–20).

What trivial excuses. No one buys a field without first looking at it. No one buys oxen without first inspecting them. Even someone newly married could bring his wife. Obviously, those invited didn't want to come. Do not confuse this group with those who attached conditions to their discipleship. At least that group offered reasons; this group just made excuses.

Many Christians today are experts in spiritual excuse-making. No matter what they are asked to do in growth or service, they respond with a spiritual-sounding excuse. Some have honed the craft to such an extent that they can claim to follow Christ while never taking more than spiritual baby steps.

Can people be disciples while constantly giving excuses for why they cannot follow Jesus? I don't think so. Basic principles of Followology demonstrate that if we're standing still, we're not following.

If we're not following, we're not followers. If our leader is moving on and we're not with him, we're just taking a walk.

In the extreme, some people try to discover the minimum amount they can follow Jesus and still be a Christian—sort of like students who only want to study what's going to be on the test. The Bible tells us nothing about minimum discipleship; instead, it challenges us to total-commitment, count-the-cost, and pay-the-price discipleship. That's the normal life of the true follower of Jesus. Exploring the opposite end of the discipleship continuum is spiritually dangerous.

ONGOING ADJUSTMENTS REQUIRED

As Christians, we should expect following Jesus to require practical adjustments in our lives. One major adjustment is how we spend our time. Discretionary time is a precious commodity. Every significant aspect of discipleship involves time. Deepening our relationship with Jesus requires time. Being involved in church requires time. Serving others in ministry requires time. In fact, time is the major currency of discipleship. As Jesus' followers, when we offer Him our lives, we are really offering Him our time. Managing our time becomes a spiritual discipline.

Another area of adjustment is how we spend our money. Nothing reveals values faster than money. As disciples of Jesus, we are called to live unselfishly. Yet we are immersed in a culture that encourages us to live beyond our means. Only when we spend less than we earn can we give to others. Chronic self-indulgence is a social problem today, but it is totally unacceptable for those who claim to follow Jesus.

A final area of adjustment focuses on our "passion." Passion refers to those things in our lives that excite us and to which we give ourselves with abandon. Many people are passionate about sports; others about their investments. Some are passionate about recreational activities. The options are endless, but the question remains: Do we care passionately about our relationship with Jesus? We have finite energy to give to life's pursuits. Too many of us squander our passion on lesser things. How can we follow Jesus fully if all we have is leftover, warmed-up passion?

THE COKE CAN MONUMENT

Discipleship offers incredible benefits—one of which we will focus on next as we dig deeper into the Relationship Principle, step five in the following process. However, we will never experience the benefits unless we pay the price—the price of paying attention to the leader, of maintaining our spiritual focus, and the price of developing an attitude of submission that enables us to adjust to our leader.

Somewhere along the side of the highway that runs northwest out of the Mojave Desert is a Coke can with teeth marks and a missing top—a small monument to an adjustment required to follow a physical leader.

Spiritually-speaking, when was the last time you bit the top off of a Coke can in your life so you could keep following Jesus?

THE SECRET OF A GREAT RELATIONSHIP

Following builds relationship.

Step #5: The Relationship Principle

The lead line of the brochure sounded promising:

"Getting around Atlanta has never been easier or less expensive than a ride on the MARTA train and bus system."

Even though MARTA is a fancy acronym for Metropolitan Atlanta Rapid Transit Authority, it sounded to me like a warm reference to a distant aunt. Great Aunt Marta. I began to feel better.

I was staying downtown in Atlanta for a week-long conference that required me to travel back and forth from my hotel to the Georgia Dome. The distance created problems. A walk in the daytime summer heat negatively impacted a business suit. A walk at night negatively impacted life expectancy. Cab fares negatively impacted financial reserves. Searching for open parking spaces negatively impacted emotional health. "No problem," my friends told me. "Just take MARTA." So, I purchased the one-week visitors' pass and began studying the directional brochure.

Great Aunt Marta turned out to be a stern old biddy who revealed directions only to those willing to grovel. The "Rapid Rail System" brochure was her tantalizing tool of torture. Folded, her list of instructions and schedules appeared to be tiny, with a front cover that measured a mere two inches by eight inches. I picked up the brochure and opened it, then opened it, then opened it, and kept opening it twelve times until it stretched in front of me—thirty-six inches by eight inches of tiny type with columns of schedules, maps, and graphics printed both horizontally and vertically on thin, white paper. Great Aunt Marta smirked.

With a growing sense of helplessness, I noticed a promising little panel of information entitled "How To Use This MARTA Timetable." Initial hope quickly evaporated as I began to read (and I quote directly from Great Aunt Marta; I am not making this up):

> To follow a bus trip you read across the page. Times are given only for certain points along the bus route called Time Points. If your departure or arrival point is between one of the Time Points, you will estimate the time the bus will be at your stop. Locate your stop on the map. Then find the nearest Time Point before your stop. Depending on which direction you wish to travel, find that Time Point on the Inbound or Outbound time section for weekdays or weekends. Estimate the number of minutes it will take the bus to get from the nearest Time Point to your stop. Then choose the time you need to travel. Letters next to times refer to important footnotes you should read. When a blank appears under a Time Point, it means that a bus does not pass by that point on that particular trip. Be at the bus stop a few minutes early and allow for errors in estimating. Shaded times are for weekend and holiday service. All times given may vary with weather and traffic conditions.[3]

I wanted to cry. Then I saw my friend Dave. "Have you used MARTA to get to the Dome?" I asked in near despair. "Sure," he said. "It's not that bad. Come on, I'll show you how it works."

Dave led me down an ominous escalator into the bowels of underground Atlanta where Great Aunt Marta reigned. He showed me how to pop my pass through the turnstile, then led me down shorter escalators to the waiting area for our first train. After a few minutes we boarded for a short ride. We got off at the next stop, rode another short escalator up to another level, and waited for a second train. Dave patiently told me where to stand and when to board. After another short ride, we reached our final station and stepped onto an ascending escalator that lifted us from the depths to the light.

Without Dave's help, I never would have deciphered the directional code and reached the Georgia Dome. But with my friend guiding me, I made the trip effortlessly. In fact, a wisp of hope suggested that I could eventually make the trip on my own. With Great Aunt Marta's laughter ringing in my ears, I quietly affirmed that it is easier to follow a leader than to follow directions. A relationship makes all the difference, which is why this part of our study of the process of following is so important.

A GREAT CASE OF THE "GET TO'S"

In the last four chapters, we've covered four of seven steps in the following process—the Need Principle, which helps build our motivation for following; the Choice Principle, which reminds us of the profound responsibility of choosing the right leader; the Focus Principle, which explains the basic discipline of following—paying attention to the leader; and the Adjustment Principle, which helps us understand the attitude of submission required in following. These four principles describe the "got to" part of following. The next three principles, though, describe the "get to" part.

There are two primary categories in life: "got to" and "get to." I've got to mow the grass; but I get to eat ice cream. I've got to exercise; but I get to go hiking in the mountains. I've got to do my taxes; but I get to read a great book.

The secret of dealing with the "got to's" is to focus on the "get to's." Most of the "get to's" depend on the "got to's." So if the "get to" is worth getting, we don't mind the "got to's." Get it?

If we want to become better followers of Jesus, there are four "got to's": (1) recognize we don't know the way; (2) choose to follow Jesus; (3) make Jesus the central focus of our lives; (4) develop a submissive attitude by adjusting our lives to whatever Jesus tells us to do. None of these "got to's" are negative, but for most of us, they don't necessarily feel like "get to's."

But there are three great "get to's": (1) if we follow Jesus, we get to develop an intimate relationship with Him; (2) if we follow Jesus, we get to experience His transforming power in our lives; and finally (3) if we follow Jesus, we get to spend eternity with Him in heaven.

In my opinion, the best of the "get to's" is our focus in this chapter —our relationship with Jesus. This relationship elevates Christianity beyond all other religions, philosophies, and worldviews. The God who created the world says we get to know Him, talk with Him, walk with

Him. In a way, God lets us "hang around" with Him. How? By following. That's how Jesus built the relationships with His first followers. By studying what He did then, we can learn how Jesus wants us to follow Him today.

Building a Following Relationship

When Jesus announced to the crowd the names of the twelve men He had selected as apostles, Mark tells us that Jesus had three objectives in mind: "He appointed twelve—designating them apostles—that they might be with him and that he might send them out to preach and to have authority to drive out demons" (Mark 3:14–15).

Jesus planned for His disciples to do something—preach. He planned to give them something—authority. But first He wanted these men to experience something—a relationship with Him. Following Him would make all of this possible.

Reading through the Gospels, it's fascinating to notice how Jesus and the disciples related to each other. Apparently, the relationship they developed involved typical steps and stages we see in any relationship. Time together became the cornerstone. Because the disciples followed Jesus, they spent enormous amounts of time with Him. Because they were with Him, open communication developed. For example, as they experienced situations in life, Jesus simply talked to His disciples and interpreted the spiritual implications of their experiences. Here is a good example: "Jesus went through all the towns and villages, teaching in their synagogues, preaching the good news of the kingdom and healing every disease and sickness. When he saw the crowds, he had compassion on them, because they were harassed and helpless, like sheep without a shepherd. Then he said to his disciples, 'The harvest is plentiful but the workers are few. Ask the Lord of the harvest, therefore, to send out workers into his harvest field'" (Matt. 9:35–38).

As a result of spending a large amount of time with Jesus, the disciples began to know how He viewed life and what He wanted them to do. Increasingly, Jesus opened His life to them. Even when the crowds pressed around Him, straining to hear His teaching and to witness His miracles, Jesus set aside private time for the disciples to ask the questions that perplexed them. "Then he left the crowd and went into the house. His disciples came to him and said, 'Explain to us the parable of the weeds in the field'" (Matt. 13:36).

Not only did the disciples need private time with Jesus to ask questions, they needed Him even more after experiencing failure in ministry. Away from the ever-present crowds, they sought solace and explanations from the only one who could provide them. "Then the disciples came to Jesus in private and asked, 'Why couldn't we drive [the demon] out?'" (Matt. 17:19).

Most days brought experiences and instruction that must have confused the disciples, but Jesus always helped them fit the jumbled pieces together. "He did not say anything to [the crowds] without using a parable. But when he was alone with his own disciples, he explained everything" (Mark 4:34).

Most good friends can point back to embarrassing things that happened that were not funny at the time but which caused red faces and laughter later. I suspect Jesus and His disciples had their share. How about Peter's comments on the Mount of Transfiguration when he didn't know what to say but went ahead and said a few things anyway. Don't forget James and John wanting to call down fire from heaven on a Samaritan village. Or what about the running argument among the disciples about which of them was the greatest. These scenes and more would have been great picks for a relational bloopers video.

Over time, Jesus shared more personal things with His disciples: more of His heart, His mission, and the weight of His calling with its inevitable cross. "They were on their way up to Jerusalem, with Jesus leading the way, and the disciples were astonished, while those who followed were afraid. Again, he took the Twelve aside and told them what was going to happen to him" (Mark 10:32).

Of course, there were tender moments together: Jesus crying at Lazarus' tomb; the Master donning slave's clothes and washing the disciples' feet; their last supper together. Yes, their relationship included intensely personal times, like the final hours they spent with Jesus in the garden of Gethsemane: "They went to a place called Gethsemane, and Jesus said to his disciples, 'Sit here while I pray.' He took Peter, James and John along with him, and he began to be deeply distressed and troubled. 'My soul is overwhelmed with sorrow to the point of death," he said to them. "Stay here and keep watch.' Going a little farther, he fell to the ground and prayed that if possible the hour might pass from him. 'Abba, Father,' he said, 'everything is possible for you. Take this cup from me. Yet not what I will, but what you will'" (Mark 14:32–36).

As often happens in relationships, there were failures: the disciples' sleeping when Jesus asked them to pray for Him; Peter's denial that He knew Jesus; Thomas's doubts.

Rather than seeing Jesus and His disciples as friends involved in a real relationship, we tend to relegate their experience to some "otherworldly" type of interaction. By placing them in a super-spiritual category, we inadvertently make it harder for us to believe we can have a "real" relationship—a friendship—with Jesus. Yet relationship is the foundational benefit of following. As His modern-day disciples, followers, and friends, Jesus has called us to be with Him. What an incredible "get to"!

Getting Back to Jesus

Obviously, we do not follow Jesus physically as His first disciples did, so how can we build our relationship with Him today? We will address this more in part 3, but for now let me offer a few suggestions that have helped me.

Start out by reading and rereading the Gospels until the facts about Jesus permeate your thinking. Set a goal of reading through all four Gospels once a month for six months. As you read, focus on how Jesus lived, not just on what He said. Pay attention to the places He went and the people He met. Work hard to see Jesus in "real time." Imagine that you were with Him as His thirteenth disciple. Envision taking those long walks with Jesus. Try to see Him; hear Him. Then capture those facts and emotions and ask Jesus to make you aware of His presence right now. Tell Him that you want to have a real relationship with Him. Tell Him that if He will help you know what He is doing around you, then you will seek to follow Him every day.

Directions in the Context of Relationship

Remember Great Aunt Marta? I'm thankful Jesus is nothing like her and that Christianity is based on a relationship rather than spiritual directions. God doesn't give us spiritual brochures that defy understanding. Thankfully, when God revealed His truth to us in written form, He didn't include disclaimers. Unlike Great Aunt Marta's erratic schedule, God's relationship with us never changes—even on weekends and holidays. Best of all, God has always known that it is easier for us to follow a leader than to follow directions, so He gave us Jesus. As we follow Jesus, we learn the way.

The next time some spiritual guru pleads with you to send a donation for his super-duper, hot-off-the-press collection of direct-from-God spiritual directions, tell him, "No thanks." Just keep following Jesus and reading *the* Book. Jesus will show you the way and teach you all the directions you need as you deepen your relationship with Him.

TOUCHED BY THE MASTER

Following changes followers.

Step #6: The Change Principle

Making guitars is no big deal. Just take some wood, pieces of metal for frets, pieces of abalone pearl for decoration, slivers of steel for strings, other assorted bits of metal and plastic, put it all in a large bag and shake vigorously, and—Shazam!—you've got a guitar.

Well . . . not exactly. At least that is not the way J. W. Gallager does it.

Most people, even serious guitar players, don't know about J. W. Gallager's guitars. Most people have never seen one since that requires a trip to the tiny town of Wartrace, Tennessee. Lots of people, though, have heard a Gallager guitar; they just don't know their favorite musicians were playing one of J. W.'s hand-crafted beauties. Those with an ear for such things claim they can recognize a Gallager guitar by the resonating, sweet tone.

How do I know so much about these guitars? I own the 2,237th guitar J. W. Gallager sold. I'll never forget the day I placed the order: September 8, 1977. That's the day J. W. gave me a crash course on guitar making and helped me appreciate the process of transforming wood, metal, abalone pearl, and plastic into a masterpiece.

After greeting me warmly in his run-down shop, J. W. led me to the display rack holding a few of his guitars. After playing various models, I knew I wanted one. All I needed to know was the price. But when I asked what they cost, J. W. suddenly became hard of hearing. "Come on back here," he said, totally ignoring my question, "and let me show you how we make these things."

I followed him to the far end of his cluttered shop to wood bins stacked with thin sheets of ash and mahogany. In guitars, J. W. explained, wood is everything. A great guitar begins with a great piece of wood—tight, even grains, no flaws. And for a truly *special* guitar, he confided, he always held back a few *special* pieces of wood.

From the wood bin, we moved from workbench to workbench as he explained each step in the long process of creating a world-class guitar. He showed me the molds used to shape the wood, one of the most time-consuming steps in the process as the wood is slowly formed into the desired shape. Rushing the process in this stage cracks the wood. Patience and time are essential.

Next we moved to another work area where J. W. and his staff assembled the bodies of the guitars by gluing wooden support braces inside in a unique pattern. From there we stopped at a workbench where they shaped the necks of the guitars, slowly transforming large blocks of wood into delicate but sturdy necks and fingerboards, topped with their distinctive S-shaped crown and adorned with the classic Gallager G.

Then on to the bench where craftsmen inlaid the abalone pearl in the fretboard and body of the top-of-the-line models—a slow, tedious process. After that came the bench where they applied multiple coats of finish to the wood, a key to the resonance and tone of the instrument.

By the time my tour was complete, I was ready to write a check. "Well, Mr. Gallager, can I buy one of these guitars and take it with me today?" I asked, pointing to the rack of guitars I had played earlier. "No," he explained, "those guitars have already been purchased and are ready to be shipped. But I can have your guitar ready in a little less than a year." One year! Incredible. Yet after seeing the process of making the guitars, I could understand why it took so long.

One minor detail remained: the price. "How much do your guitars cost?" I asked. Confidently, J. W. Gallager handed me a price list. I swallowed, trying not to gasp. I focused initially on one of the mid-range guitars. Mentally calculating my savings, I chose one I could afford with a financial stretch. That was not, however, what I really wanted. I hesitated. Finally, taking a deep breath, I asked, "Mr. Gallager, how much does one of those *special* guitars cost, one you make with the special wood and the abalone pearl?" He named the price. Then I did gasp!

Months later, UPS delivered my top-of-the-line Gallager 71 *Special*, number 2,237. Pasted inside the guitar was a handwritten note: "Made especially for John Kramp by J. W. Gallager." The master guitar-maker had plied his craft, and the transformation process was complete. I strummed a cord, listened as the resonating tone rang, and marveled that a pile of wood and materials could become a beautiful instrument. As I studied the invoice, which included the date I placed my order and the price I had paid, I realized how slow and costly transformation can be.

TRANSFORMED BY FOLLOWING JESUS

In the sixth step of the following process, we seek to understand the Change Principle. I believe change is the primary purpose for following. Certainly there are other purposes as well. Following enables us to develop a relationship with our leader as we saw in the last chapter. And as we will see in the next chapter, following promises a reward— the destination we share with our leader. Yet Christianity emphasizes the incredible power that God unlocks in our lives when we choose to follow Jesus. As followologists seeking to understand how to become better followers of Jesus, the stories about Jesus' disciples become wonderful prototypes of this change process and provide a benchmark for what is possible through God's power.

Anyone who knew Jesus' first followers before they met Jesus— their families, neighbors, friends—must have marveled at what happened to them. They could never forget who these men were, so they never stopped being amazed at who the disciples became. We must do the same thing, connecting the accounts of their lives in the Gospels with record of their transformation in the Book of Acts.

Certainly the disciples had some admirable qualities from the beginning. They did respond to Jesus' invitation, leaving family and vocation to follow Him. Their response to Him reveals a measure of interest in spiritual things, although we are never sure if their motivation centered more on political self-interests than on spiritual goals. Yet we can affirm the fact that they joined Jesus on His mission.

Reading the Gospels, however, we discover that these men were not spiritual superheroes. They struggled with ambition, fear, rivalry, prejudice—all the ills that plague most of us. Many times, Jesus had to teach them spiritual truths repeatedly before they understood and even longer before they applied the truths to their lives. In the end, they all failed Jesus—deserting Him, denying Him, betraying Him. Even after

Jesus rose from the dead, the disciples continued to ask questions about when He would set up His political kingdom. Apparently, they still didn't get it.

Frankly, I'm glad they didn't. I'm thankful for every one of their struggles. Every time their faith failed, I take heart. Every time they bickered and jockeyed for position, I take comfort. When they could not understand spiritual truths that should have been clear, I grin. And when they fail miserably at the critical moment when Jesus needed their support the most, I sigh with relief. Why? Because all these things convince me that they are just like me, like us.

Reading about spiritual superheroes is interesting, but it can be demotivating. If the disciples had started out strong and followed Jesus without faltering, we could admire them but would probably struggle to identify with them. Frankly, I'm glad the disciples messed up as much as they did. Because of their struggles, the positive changes that took place in their lives hold promise for all of us. Their story of transformation becomes our story.

THE AFTER PART OF "BEFORE AND AFTER"

If the Gospels and the Book of Acts were a photo album, the Gospels would be the "before" shots, and Acts would contain the "after" shots. My favorite "after" shot is found in Acts 4. Because of the powerful preaching of the apostles in Jerusalem and the miracles they performed, the number of believers in the city grew to more than five thousand. This posed a serious threat to the religious establishment. So the rulers, elders, and teachers of the law had Peter and John arrested and imprisoned. Later, they brought them before the council and demanded to know by what power they were doing all that was being done. Peter's response was classic:

> Then Peter, filled with the Holy Spirit, said to them: "Rulers and elders of the people! If we are being called to account today for an act of kindness shown to a cripple and are asked how he was healed, then know this, you and all the people of Israel: It is by the name of Jesus Christ of Nazareth, whom you crucified but whom God raised from the dead, that this man stands before you healed. He is 'the

stone you builders rejected, which has become the cap-
stone.' Salvation is found in no one else, for there is no
other name under heaven given to men by which we must
be saved." (Acts 4:8–12)

Not bad for the guy who had denied that he even knew Jesus a few
weeks earlier! Something had happened. Those listening to Peter
groped for an answer and came up with only one: "When they saw the
courage of Peter and John and realized that they were unschooled, ordinary men, they were astonished and they took note that these men had
been with Jesus" (Acts 4:13).

The cumulative impact of following Jesus for those years had
reached critical mass. When the Holy Spirit energized that knowledge
and experience, the disciples became people who bore little resem-
blance to the people they had been. For those who knew these men
before, the only explanation for who they had become was Jesus—they
had been following Jesus.

HOPE FOR A CHANGE

People wonder if they can become something other than what they are.
Can people change? Or are we trapped by the forces that have shaped
our lives, fenced in by conditioning and genetics, crippled by social
forces and innate abilities? In the quest for change, people search desperately, chasing fads and hanging on the words of discredited
prophets. In contrast, Jesus offers hope for real change. Not a flash-in-
the-pan, hope-it-lasts change, but a foundational shift in how we relate
to our Creator. The apostle Paul, someone who experienced a dramatic
personal change in his life, expressed this promise of change this way:
"Therefore, if anyone is in Christ, he is a new creation; the old has
gone, the new has come!" (2 Cor. 5:17).

In the language of Lostology and Followology, when we are "in
Christ," we get found. Rather than being spiritually lost, we are finally
where we are supposed to be—with the God who loves us. That means
that our old experience of being spiritually lost is gone and our new
experience of being spiritually found has begun. Having been found, we
can never be lost from God again. Yet "getting found" or being "in
Christ" is only the beginning. The old experience of following our own

instincts or the best hunches of others is gone. Now "in Christ" we have the new experience of following Jesus and opening our lives to His progressive work of change in us. That is the Christian life. What a message of hope for a world that wonders if change is possible. All they need is the touch of the Master's hand.

TOUCHED BY A MASTER

In 1973, I heard a poem written by Myra Brooks Welch, something she had written in the early 1900s. Her words painted a scene in my mind that moved me deeply. Later, I discovered her poem was well known and had been used in sermons for years. I found a copy of the words and began working with them, adapting, rewriting, weaving lyrics with an emerging melody. The first time I performed the song "The Touch of the Master's Hand," I sensed that God had allowed me to be part of a unique work of art—a message first given to a lady I never met, complemented with new words and a melody God placed in my heart. Unfortunately, my attempts to find someone to record the song failed, and I gave up. I put the song in my file cabinet and forgot about it. Almost a decade later, a young Christian musician called me requesting permission to include the song on his first album. His name is Wayne Watson. His recording of "The Touch of the Master's Hand" reached the "number one" spot on the Christian recording charts and has continued to be sung and recorded by others since then.

Looking back, it is fitting that a song that tells of the Master's touch would require that touch in its transformation process from old poem to unknown song tucked in a file cabinet to a song recorded by a top Christian recording artist. The Master's touch always transforms the ordinary. That touch proclaims the potential trapped inside common things and unimpressive people. Potential, though, can be released. Under the skilled hand of the Master, change becomes possible—not instant change; rather, metamorphosis. What "is" slowly becomes "what can be." Perhaps that's why the poem by Myra Brooks Welch and the song recorded by Wayne Watson continue to encourage people today. We all want to change, to become different people, better people. The Master makes that possible. We see it clearly in the radical transformation that took place in the lives of Jesus' first followers. The good news for us is that the Master continues to touch and transform all who follow Him today. As you read the following lyrics, why not ask the Master to transform your life as you follow Him? He will.

THE TOUCH OF THE MASTER'S HAND

It was battered and scarred and the auctioneer thought it scarcely worth his while to waste much time on the old violin so he held it up with a smile. "It sure ain't much but it's all we got left; I guess we ought to sell it, too. Who'll start the bid on this old violin? Just one more and we'll be through."

Then he cried out, "One give me one dollar. Who'll make it two? Only two dollars. Who'll make it three? Three dollars twice, now that's a good price, but who's got a bid for me? Raise up your hand; don't wait any longer. The auction's about to end. Who's got four, just one dollar more to bid on this old violin?"

The air was hot and the people stood round as the sun was setting low. From the back of the crowd a gray-haired man came forward and picked up the bow. He wiped the dust from the old violin and he tightened up the strings. Then he played out a melody pure and sweet, as sweet as an angel sings.

Then the music stopped and the auctioneer with a voice that was quiet and low. "Now what am I bid for this old violin?" as he held it up with the bow.

Then he cried out, "One, give me one thousand. Who'll make it two? Only two thousand. Who'll make it three? Three thousand twice. Now that's a good price, but who's got a bid for me?" The people called out, "What made the change? We don't understand." The auctioneer stopped then he said with a smile, "It was the touch of the master's hand."

Well many a man with life out of tune is battered and scarred by sin. And he's auctioned cheap to a thankless world, much like that old violin. But the Master comes and the foolish crowd never understands the worth of soul and the change that's wrought by the touch of the Master's hand.[4]

Why do we follow Jesus? In part because following Jesus changes us. As we follow, the Master touches our lives and slowly makes us what we always dreamed we could be.

Why is the change process slow and costly? Just ask J. W. Gallager. Starting with the pile of wood, he will take you step by step through the process that ends with a world-class guitar. When he is done, you will understand why the final product takes longer to complete and costs more.

Why is the change process slow and costly? Just ask Jesus. Starting with a group of ordinary people, He will take you step by step through the process that ends with world-class Christians. When He is done, you will understand why the final product takes longer to complete and costs more.

Over time and for a price, world-class guitars are made.

Over time and for a price, people become world-class followers of Jesus.

Understand the process and you understand why.

WHEN YOU GET WHERE YOU'RE GOING, YOU'RE THERE

11

*Followers go where
their leaders are going.*

Step #7: The Destination Principle

We dropped our packs and climbed the short distance to the ridge. "The Tooth of Time" welcomed us as it had so many boys before. The bare-rock protrusion stood sentry over Philmont Scout Ranch— 137,493 acres in the northeast corner of New Mexico, part of the Sangre de Cristo range of the Rockies. Tales of this ancient rock had gripped our imaginations during the months of preparation for our trip. Faint glimpses of the rocky ridge during our fourteen-day wilderness trek had steeled our resolve to conquer the summit. Finally we lined the ridge, reveling in our accomplishment. A motley crew—a dirty dozen middle school boys flanked by our exhausted leaders.

For days we had trudged over rugged terrain at elevations from 6,500 to 12,441 feet. Traveling four to eight miles each day with forty-pound backpacks, we had endured an array of challenges: blistered feet, ice-cold showers, daily thunderstorms, nighttime temperatures that dropped to forty degrees and below, foraging bears with a sweet tooth, one-log bridges across gullies and streams, and dehydrated trail food that defied description and, at times, consumption.

In spite of everything, we persevered and climbed, moving ever closer to "The Tooth of Time." Once there, we gazed over the eastern plains of New Mexico and looked down with longing on Tent City in Base Camp, our final destination. Our view from the ridge punctuated our wilderness adventure with an exclamation point.

Although we did not understand it at the time, our adventure had unfolded according to the time-tested, seven-step following process. As

63

inexperienced backpackers, we understood the Need Principle. We didn't know where we were going, so we were highly motivated to follow someone who knew the way. The Choice Principle forced us to choose the leaders we would follow on our high-country odyssey, and we were responsible for our choice. The Focus Principle continually challenged us and led naturally to the Adjustment Principle as we struggled to keep our leaders in sight and move at their pace up steep trails and never-ending switchbacks. Along the way, we discovered the Relationship Principle. Campers and leaders alike developed friendships that didn't exist before; shared pain forged lasting memories. And even though some people doubted it was possible, our dirty dozen did experience the Change Principle. Philmont changed us from inexperienced trekkers to "veterans" . . . well, that would be pushing it. Finally, we added the last link in the following chain: the Destination Principle; in our case, "The Tooth of Time." From day one, our leaders had told us we would reach the summit. We stayed with them and in time found ourselves lining the rocky ridge.

I wish I could tell you what we did on "The Tooth of Time." We had discussed it for days and anticipated that one defining moment. Fortunately, there were no cameras. I will leave that "photo" to your imagination. But even boyish nonsense eventually gave way to reflection. There from that bare-rock ridge, pockmarked by thousands of lightning strikes, boys and leaders surveyed where we had been and took satisfaction in how far we had come.

So it is for us as spiritual followers of Jesus Christ. Although the destination is not our primary motivation for discipleship, the things to come help us now. True discipleship is a long walk the following way. The road is not easy; it is an arduous journey with many changes in fortune. In spite of what happens along the way, the destination is sure.

Thus far in our study of the seven-step following process, we have focused on two of the three benefits of being a wise follower: our relationship with our leader, and the changes that experience brings to our lives. In this chapter, we're going to examine the final benefit, the destination, and seek to understand how it caps the entire process. The Destination Principle describes the reward for following and reveals a foundational followism illustrated in this story.

One foggy night in England, an American businessman traveled on a narrow, two-lane road. Since he was unfamiliar with the area, he was apprehensive about his ability to find his destination. Heavy fog cut visibility almost to zero. He slowed the car and peered desperately into the darkness.

Suddenly, a car emerged from the rear, passed him, and moved ahead rapidly into the darkness. "Surely," the businessman thought, "a driver going that fast in this fog must know the way. If I can follow him, I'll make it back to the city."

He increased his speed until he saw the red taillights of the car that had passed him. Fixing his gaze on those lights, he accelerated, turned, slowed, and curved exactly as that car did. As the fog grew even more dense, he moved even closer to the lead car, never allowing distance to build between them.

Some time later, the lead car stopped without warning. The businessman slammed on his brakes, but still smashed into the rear of the car he had followed. In frustration and anger, he stepped out of the car just as the driver of the lead car came toward him.

"Hey, fellow," the American said, "why don't you signal and give folks a little warning before you come to a dead stop like that?"

The Englishman retorted, "Sir, I didn't think it was necessary. You see, it *is* my garage."

Whether we follow physically or follow spiritually, we experience this followism: Followers go where their leaders are going. Faithfully following yields a reward: the destination. The destination in no way minimizes the journey and the full range of experiences involved but, like icing on a cake, the destination tops off the entire process. For that reason, we are not surprised that Jesus emphasized the spiritual destination of discipleship.

A Destination to Come

After following Jesus for more than three years, the disciples spent what would be their final night with Jesus—a night of tenderness but confusion. Before serving the Passover meal, their Master washed their feet as if He were a common slave. Later, He warned of a betrayer and a denial. Then He dropped the emotional bombshell that left the disciples convulsing with confusion: "Do not let your hearts be troubled. Trust in God; trust also in me. In my Father's house are many rooms; if it were not so, I would have told you. I am going there to prepare a place for you. And if I go and prepare a place for you, I will come back and take you to be with me that you also may be where I am. You know the way to the place where I am going" (John 14:1–4).

Going away? Had they heard Him correctly? In spite of Jesus' exhortation, fear conquered their hearts. The fact that He would prepare a place for them mattered little, for they focused on one thing: He was going to a place they could not come—at least not yet. They could not grasp that their leader was simply moving farther ahead so He could arrive first and complete preparations. In time, they would join Him. Followers always share destinations with their leaders. None of this, however, quieted their hearts.

Where was this place, this mysterious destination? Jesus described it to them as He had before, but language failed to translate the spiritual realities into common terms. So Jesus sketched the destination in their minds with word pictures and analogies.

- Their destination would be a wonderful place where spiritual treasures would be stored and never destroyed (Matt. 6:20).

- There, all the world's peoples from east and west would join in a feast with Abraham, Isaac, and Jacob (Matt. 8:11).

- The place He prepared for them would exceed all expectations, like the growth of a mustard seed or the work of yeast in dough (Matt. 13:31,33).

- The destination would have incalculable value—like a treasure hidden in a field or a pearl of great price (Matt. 13:44–45).

- Yet the place He prepared could be found easily with a child's faith while remaining invisible to proud eyes (Matt. 18:3–4).

Jesus tried to help His disciples understand the preparations He would make for them, but they struggled to comprehend. They had not been where He was going. They did not know the way. They only knew Him, but that was not enough—or so they thought. "Thomas said to him, 'Lord, we don't know where you are going, so how can we know the way?' Jesus answered, 'I am the way and the truth and the life. No one comes to the Father except through me'" (John 14:5–6).

Jesus understood their confusion but stilled their hearts with one constant in the midst of change: I am the way; if you know Me, you know the way. Years later, the writer of Hebrews would encourage other Christians with the same counsel: "Therefore, since we are surrounded by such a great cloud of witnesses, let us throw off everything that hinders and the sin that so easily entangles, and let us run with perseverance the race marked out for us. Let us fix our eyes on Jesus, the author and perfecter of our faith, who for the joy set before him endured the cross, scorning its shame, and sat down at the right hand of the throne of God. Consider him who endured such opposition from sinful men, so that you will not grow weary and lose heart" (Heb. 12:1–3).

As we face uncertainty or when discouragement wearies us, we must fix our spiritual eyes again on Jesus, our leader who endured a cross on the way to His destination. More than any other words and images, those of Hebrews 12:1–3 have encouraged me as I've traveled my road of discipleship. When the goal of becoming a better follower of Jesus has felt elusive, I've used this passage to set my eyes again on Him. Years ago, I wrote a song based on these verses. Perhaps my words will help you see the inspired words from Hebrews in a new way.

The Runners Song

A lone runner ran down a dusty road. His body ached from the weight of his load. Dreams of the finish line seemed to explode for the race was far too long. "I can run no more," he said with a cry, but just at that moment a man ran by. He matched the pace of the runner's stride and began to sing this song.

"Run—keep on running. You'll finish the race. Fix your eyes on me and then I'll set the pace. Cast off anything that will hinder you. Run for your race is almost through."

With those words the man pulled ahead. The runner thought of the words he'd said, but soon his gaze was drawn instead to the body of the man. For his feet were maimed from an awful blow; his hands were marred by a wound long ago. And with each stride the pain would show but the man still sang the song.

"Run—keep on running. You'll finish the race. Fix your eyes on me and then I'll set the pace. Cast off anything that will hinder you. Run for your race is almost through."

They topped a hill and there below stood a coliseum grand where the greatest runners of all time were seated in the stands. As they entered in the crowd began to urge them round the field. In the song they sang, the man's name rang, his majesty revealed.

"Run—keep on running. You'll finish the race. Fix your eyes on Jesus. Let Him set the pace. Cast off anything that will hinder you. Run for your race is almost through."

Jesus ran so we follow Him. We compete as those who know they'll win. The prize awaits God's champions—the faithful who endure. For with each step He's by our side. Those who have gone before look on in pride. We'll end our race and come inside to join the runner's song![5]

Can you hear Jesus exhorting you to keep running? Can you hear the chorus from all who have followed Jesus before you? They call your name and mine, pleading with us to complete the course and join their collective song of encouragement to all who follow later. A destination awaits us, one prepared by the one we follow. But is the destination simply a reward to keep us performing desired spiritual activities? No, heaven simply tops off the other benefits of discipleship we begin experiencing on earth.

For all of eternity we will continue to enjoy our relationship with Him—a relationship enriched by our experiences of following Him on earth. In heaven, we will finally be formed and fashioned fully into His image, but following Jesus on earth is part of that ultimate transformation process. Yet heaven is not for us, not really. Author Joni Eareckson Tada, a quadriplegic crippled in her teens in a diving accident, speaks of this eloquently in her book *Heaven, Your Real Home*.

In the early days of my paralysis when I first learned about heaven, I zeroed in on it because it was the place where I would receive new hands and feet. Heaven was the place I'd be freed from the pain, and so, it became an escape from reality. A psychological crutch. At times, heaven was so me-centered that I felt as though the whole point of it was to get back all it owed me, all I had lost. And so, heaven became a death wish.

Time passed, and with it I gained a little more spiritual maturity. It gradually dawned on me that the Day of Christ would be just that . . . the Day of Christ, not the day of Joni. Glorified hands and feet, as well as reunion with loved ones, began to look more like fringe benefits to the honor of simply being on the invitation list to the coronation party.

You'll agree. The privilege of casting your crowns at the feet of Jesus will be enough of an honor. Ruling the earth and reigning over angels, becoming pillars in God's temple and co-heirs of heaven and earth are almost incidental. What we become, receive, and do in heaven won't be the highlight of heaven. To be there and to be the praise of His glory will be enough. It will be Jesus' Day.[6]

THE INEVITABLE ENDING EITHER WAY

Of course, the "following" process works the same way if we follow the wrong leader. If we choose an evil leader, we still end up where that leader is going. The writer of Proverbs counseled against such folly: "There is a way that seems right to a man, but in the end it leads to death" (Prov. 14:12).

Whether we become wise followers or foolish followers, we will reach a destination. There, at the end of the line, we find our reward, the culmination of the choices made and the path followed. All we have to do is follow the leader.

Many forces, though, will obstruct our commitment to follow Jesus. Fortunately, we have an advantage. As followologists, we can anticipate the types of obstacles we will encounter and can take steps to deal with them. In part 3, we will learn about these discipleship obstacles and develop a strategy for going over them, around them, or through them. We must follow. For now, we can take heart from an old story about a fox chasing a rabbit across an open field.

A farmer sat on the fence and observed the fox gaining ground on the rabbit. He called out, "From where I am, it looks like you ain't gonna make it, Mr. Rabbit." The rabbit called back, "From where I am, I ain't got no choice. So I'm planning to make it." And so he did.

And so will we. Fixing our eyes on Jesus, the author and perfecter of our faith, we will make it. We will reach the destination He has prepared for us.

III

STEPPING OVER THE FOLLOWING OBSTACLES

Followism 12:   If you're the follower, you're not the leader.
   ▶ Obstacle #1: Role Confusion

Followism 13:   Followers always need their leaders.
   ▶ Obstacle #2: Spiritual Pride

Followism 14:   People follow in different ways.
   ▶ Obstacle #3: Comparing Yourself to Other
      Followers

Followism 15:   Sometimes it's hard to follow.
   ▶ Obstacle #4: Unrealistic Expectations

Followism 16:   Testing while following enhances learning.
   ▶ Obstacle #5: Misunderstanding the Purpose
      of Testing

Followism 17:   Those who fail can follow again.
   ▶ Obstacle #6: Failure

71

THE ROLE OF A LIFETIME

12

*If you're the follower,
you're not the leader.*

Obstacle #1: Role Confusion

Ten-year-old Kevin has had a hard life. As the little brother in a family with two older sisters, he has fought to be his own man and struggled to express his individuality. Mandy and Jenny, his older sisters, have tried to control his life. They mean no harm. They simply do what big sisters are predestined to do to little brothers.

On one occasion, they gave Kevin orders and expected him to obey. When he resisted, all parties exchanged ideas with escalating volume. Like tag-team wrestlers, Mandy and Jenny ganged up in a unified show of big-sisterly force. Pinned to the mat for the count, Kevin used his secret weapon. In a voice racked with pain but laced with defiance, he called to his parents: "Mandy and Jenny are 'momming' me again."

Momming? The look on his parents' faces revealed that this was not the first time the sisters had been accused of "momming" Kevin. With a grimace and eye-roll, Karen (the real mom) called, "Mandy! Jenny! You're not the mom. Leave Kevin alone."

It was a classic case of role confusion, a contagious disease that infects most families—including mine. On a regular basis, my daughters resist a "mom-ultimatum." After a brief verbal skirmish with predictable results, my wife, Lynn Marie, ends debate by clarifying the roles. "Look," she says, "you're not the mom. You're the kids. I'm the mom. Got it?" Our girls get it, because if they don't, they know they're going to "get it."

Role confusion is certainly not limited to the parent-child relationship. Similar tensions exist between leaders and followers. In fact, role confusion is the first of six "following obstacles" we will learn to identify and avoid.

EHPECTATIONS NOT ON TARGET

Ask committed Christians if they understand that Jesus is the leader instead of them and they will give you an odd look and say, "Well of course Jesus is the leader." Yet if we believe this, why do we live as if we're in charge of our lives so much of the time? The root problem may be role confusion—a subtle problem we see clearly in Jesus' first disciples. Fortunately, we can learn from their mistakes.

Problems began for the disciples soon after they began following Jesus. In the first chapter of Mark, we learn about dramatic events that took place in the city of Capernaum. During one long day of ministry, Jesus taught in the synagogue where He cast out a demon from a man, healed Simon's mother-in-law from a fever, then healed and cast out demons as the entire town gathered outside the home where He was staying. Needless to say, things were going well for the fledgling ministry, and Jesus' disciples were excited. When they awoke the next morning, a crowd waited outside, clamoring for more. The disciples turned to Jesus and . . . well, they couldn't find Him. Not anywhere. They searched. No Jesus. They left the house, scouring the surrounding area hoping to find where He had gone. Some time later, they discovered where He was and what He was doing. They were not pleased. "Very early in the morning, while it was still dark, Jesus got up, left the house and went off to a solitary place, where he prayed. Simon and his companions went to look for him, and when they found him, they exclaimed: 'Everyone is looking for you!'" (Mark 1:35–37).

That is what the disciples said. Here's what they *wanted* to say according to the KUV—the *Kramp Uninspired Version:* "Jesus, will you knock off this praying business. All that is fine for the off-hours, but this is show time. We've got a crowd back here and they are rocking and stomping. This thing is big. We've got everything set up for you. The crowds are pumped. You're up!"

Strange thing, though. Jesus was unimpressed. He responded succinctly with words that left no room for argument: "Jesus replied, 'Let us go somewhere else—to the nearby villages—so I can preach there also. That is why I have come.' So he traveled throughout

Galilee, preaching in their synagogues and driving out demons"
(Mark 1:38–39).

For the disciples, the entire experience must have been extremely
confusing. Their actions and comments suggest that although they had
agreed to follow Jesus, they had certain expectations about what that
experience would entail. From their perspective, their expectations
were not unrealistic in light of all they had given up to follow Jesus.
Simply stated, they thought Jesus should follow their schedule, accomplish their agenda, reach their destination, and love the right people.
That's all.

But Jesus torpedoed the whole plan. First He disregarded their
schedule. He was off praying somewhere at the prime time the crowds
were gathering. As a result, the momentum from the previous night
was lost. Then, Jesus dismissed their agenda and left the crowds waiting. How could He do that? the disciples must have thought. There
were sick people back there; people possessed by demons; people who
needed Him. The disciples had the whole day planned for Him, and
Jesus blew it. To make matters worse, Jesus didn't consult with them
about the itinerary. They wanted to take the show on the road and play
the big venues, but Jesus simply started walking down the road. Crisis
point. Decision time. The disciples had to stay put or follow. To make
matters worse, Jesus refused to love the right people. The disciples had
a perfectly good crowd of Jews waiting for Him. But no! Jesus went to
other towns—including some in Samaria! He had no standards.
Samaritans. Women. Even Gentiles. Jesus loved all of them. The disciples were aghast.

After awhile the truth became clear to the disciples: Jesus was the
leader. As a result, He kept the schedule He wanted to keep. He did
what He wanted to do. He went where He wanted to go. He loved
whoever He met. Bottom line: Jesus led and expected His disciples to
follow.

Following the Father's Agenda

What they would learn later was that Jesus moved in lockstep with
directives from the Heavenly Father. In reality, Jesus kept the Father's
schedule, followed the Father's agenda, went where the Father sent
Him, and loved everyone the Father brought His way. Years later, after

Jesus' ascension, the disciples would follow Jesus in the same way He had followed the Father. But Jesus knew that lesson was more than they could bear as novice followers. So He simply kept moving forward and bringing them to decision points every day. Every morning when Jesus walked down the road, He clarified the roles once again.

It is easy for us to snicker at the disciples' audacity. Imagine them thinking they were the leaders and that Jesus should conform to their expectations. But most of us do the same thing. As I have become more sensitive to Jesus' leadership role in my life, I've seen how easily I chafe against my role as His follower. You see, I'm a schedule, agenda, and itinerary kind of guy. I make plans and accomplish tasks. Sure, I like people but prefer people to fit into the time slot I allocate. Interruptions bother me because they interfere with my plans. People trash my schedule, send my agendas topsy-turvy, and keep me from reaching my goals. As you might guess, God has been confronting me on this point and reminding me (in not-so-subtle ways) about my role.

God chose one especially jam-packed week for my Followology lab work. His tool was my relationship with an international friend I'll call Kim Lee. Kim was completing a graduate degree, so he and his family lived in Nashville for two years. My wife and I enjoy working with internationals, but at times it creates unexpected demands on our lives. When Kim called me, I sensed that one of those demanding times was about to begin.

Kim was an intelligent, self-sufficient individual who made decisions and led others. He was extremely conscientious about my time and hesitated to ask for my help for fear of inconveniencing me. So when he called late one night and explained that he had decided to find a new place for his family to live, I knew he *really* needed my help. As he explained his need, my words assured him that I would help, but my heart twisted and my stomach churned. Instantly, my schedule and agenda disintegrated. During the week that followed, I devoted hours to helping him make calls, find out about schools, and evaluate alternatives. In the end, they found a beautiful place to live and were extremely happy and grateful for my help. But the practical consequences remained for me. Projects were behind schedule, items were not marked off my agenda, and completing longer-range goals seemed even less likely.

So why did I stop the good things I was doing to help Kim? Because I believe God placed Kim in my life at that time to accomplish something significant—in Kim's life and in mine. Initially, Lynn Marie and I were not excited when we discovered we would be "host family" through Vanderbilt University for a Korean family. One of our goals in working with internationals is to have the opportunity to share Christ, especially with people who have been closed to the gospel in their countries. Since so many Koreans are Christians, we could not understand why God had led Kim and his family to us.

Shortly after we met them, we learned why. After dinner in our home, Kim and I sat in my study. We were still getting acquainted and the language barrier made communication challenging. I told him about my work in publishing and writing and explained that I wrote books about the Bible. He looked at me and said, "I am not a Christian. Some time, I like to talk with you about this book."

While Kim and I were talking, Lynn Marie was struggling to communicate with his wife, who I'll call Jin. Her English was limited, but she obviously wanted to tell Lynn Marie something important and desperately wanted her to understand. Jin said she was a Christian and that her children were Christians but that Kim was not a Christian. She had been praying for him for ten years. She believed God had led them to America and to us so that I would talk to Kim about Jesus. In fact, she had called her pastor in Korea, told him about us, and asked him to pray that Kim would become a Christian while in America.

Obviously, I was stunned. Months later Kim's parents came to visit, and we enjoyed a wonderful visit and a Korean feast. Before we left that night, Kim's father took me aside and said, "My son is not a Christian. I am a Christian. I know you are a Christian, and I am praying that you will help my son become a Christian."

There are times when God's work is so clear that even I recognize it. This was one of those times. I knew that God had orchestrated events and brought Kim around the world so that he could learn about Jesus. In this case, Kim knew information about Jesus, and we talked about spiritual things. But I sensed that God wanted to use my willingness to serve Kim to help him understand Christ's love. So when Kim called to ask for help finding a new home, I knew that although he had dialed the phone, God had directed the call. God was leading; my role was to follow. So I scrapped my schedule and agenda and tried to follow—what Lynn Marie and I laughingly called my Korean real estate ministry.

God used that experience to clarify my expectations in discipleship once again. God is in control and expects me to follow the schedule He sets, work on the agenda He creates, go to the places He determines, and allow people into my life when He sends them my way. The lessons are not easy for me. They never have been. But the lessons are good.

THE FOLLY OF ROLE REVERSAL

Of all the obstacles that keep us from becoming better followers of Jesus, none is more treacherous than role confusion. On the surface, it sounds so simple: Jesus is the leader; we are the followers. But knowing that theological fact and living that discipleship truth are vastly different. As Christians, we should begin every day by affirming this truth: "Jesus is the leader; I am the follower. My goal today is to follow His schedule, accomplish His agenda, reach His destination, and love whoever He sends my way."

That is true discipleship. Anything else or anything less is folly. In fact, it reminds me of my first meeting with Domenikos Theotokopoulous. Actually, my wife and I both met him when Dr. William Hendricks introduced us. You may not know either man. Domenikos Theotokopoulous has been dead for 350 years, and Dr. Hendricks is a . . . well, it's difficult to describe him in a single word. Let me simply tell you what happened.

Domenikos Theotokopoulous, also known as El Greco, is hailed by scholars as one of the greatest painters in history. So when an exhibit of his masterpieces came to the Dallas Art Museum, the critics, the curious, the students, and casual observers came to glimpse spiritual and religious truth through the eyes and soul of El Greco. That is why Lynn Marie and I joined Dr. Hendricks at the museum.

After entering the first gallery, we watched in amusement as Dr. Hendricks stepped close to one massive painting, examining each element and probing each secret. Satisfied, he turned to us and began telling El Greco's story. "Did you notice this?" he said, pointing to an intricate symbol. "This is how we know this is . . ." Then Dr. Hendricks launched into an animated and expansive explanation of Christian history as captured on El Greco's canvas. Our questions prompted further explanations. One historical anecdote triggered another, his voice resonating with increased volume.

Other people eased closer so they could listen. In time, they began asking questions. Our group of three began to grow. Another gallery. Another painting. More additions to our group. Dr. Hendricks didn't walk; he flowed. His words, his gestures, his voice filled the air. As he renewed his personal relationship with El Greco, he shared thoughts in a stream of consciousness with his growing entourage.

"Who is that man?" people asked. "Does he work for the museum?" "No," I responded with amusement, "he's a seminary professor. He wanted to see the exhibit, so my wife and I brought him."

For more than two hours, our class of strangers moved and listened. As we reached the final gallery, the museum staff watched in puzzled silence. With gentle finality, Dr. Hendricks dismissed his class by saying, "You won't mind if I walk through one more time on my own and drink in the ambiance." With that, he returned to the galleries for a private session with his friend, Domenikos Theotokopoulous.

Let me ask you a question. In the museum that day, who established the schedule? Who set the agenda? Who determined the destination? Who decided who could join our group? In short, who was the leader?

Obviously, Dr. Hendricks was the leader. People followed because they recognized he knew the way. He was the authority. But what if I had become jealous of the attention Dr. Hendricks was getting and began competing with him, standing in front of one of El Greco's masterpieces while sharing my insights with the group? No way. No one would have stopped following Dr. Hendricks to follow me—at least not for long!

As disciples we should ask God to remind us every day how silly it is for us to think we are the leaders. Being the follower is a wonderful role, a role to celebrate, the role of a lifetime. Repeat after me: Jesus is the leader; I am the follower. Got it? Good. Live every day with that profound truth in mind and you'll take a giant step forward in becoming a better follower of Jesus.

13

THE
GREATEST EVER

*Followers always
need their leaders.*

Obstacle #2: Spiritual Pride
The doctor tilted my head back and shone a penlight up my left nostril. "You have a deviated septum," he said. "Do you remember anything that might have caused that? A blow of some sort?"

Although the incident happened more than three decades ago, I can recall it in detail and know who to blame. My father. An extended, escalating argument led to a permanent alteration of my nose. Now after all these years, I'm ready to tell the story and let you decide who was at fault.

It happened at Lake Texoma in north Texas where our family spent time when I was growing up. In addition to fishing and swimming, my favorite activity was waterskiing. I was good. I knew I was good. I expected others to acknowledge that I was good. At thirteen, my vocational goal was to become a professional water-skier at Cyprus Gardens in Florida. How did I develop such skiing prowess, you ask? My father. A strain in that teacher-student relationship led to the argument.

My father taught me how to ski—a fascinating fact since he has never skied in his life and taught me without ever getting in the water. When I became interested in the sport, he researched it, talked to skiers and teachers, then worked with me for endless hours until I achieved superior skills. One feat eluded me, though, and I determined that I would master it—beach landing.

I had watched other skiers race up and down the beach behind fast boats until they captured the crowd's attention. Then they cut the wake one final time, picked up speed, turned loose of the rope, and skimmed across the water until their ski tip slid onto the sandy shore.

Then as a finale, they stepped gracefully out of the ski and onto the beach to a chorus of praise and admiration. As a self-absorbed adolescent, that appealed to all my hot-dog instincts. I craved the attention, the adulation of the people on the beach (especially the cute girls!). Nothing would deter me from reaching my goal—except my father.

For days I pleaded with him to help me master the technique, but he resisted. He worried about safety. Nonsense, I thought. When he finally consented to let me try the maneuver, he sabotaged me. Since he controlled the speed of the boat and the distance from the shore, I was dependent on him. Over and over, my quest for the perfect beach landing failed as I ran out of speed and sunk before reaching the sandy shoreline. After each failure, I berated my father as only a thirteen-year-old can do for not going faster or closer to the shore. Finally, he had enough. In spite of his warnings and concerns, he did it my way.

The setting was perfect. Swimmers, sun bathers, and plenty of cute girls packed the beach. The lack of wind left the water glassy-smooth. After racing up and down the beach a few times to draw attention, I prepared for my grand, show-stopping finish. I signaled for my father to head toward the shore. He did as instructed: full speed, up close. At the optimum moment, I cut the wake for maximum speed and went skimming across the water, straining on the rope until the last possible moment, then throwing it high into the air for dramatic effect, balancing on one ski and shooting for the shore.

Objectively speaking, it was impressive. People watched, awestruck by my skill. It was a moment of glory. Unfortunately, it was an Eveready Bunny moment that kept going, and going, and going.

Rather than losing speed as I approached the beach, my speed remained high. Not only did the tip of my ski reach the shore, my entire ski sliced through the hot sand until the rudder dug deep and lodged. Although my ski stopped, the laws of physics did not, and my body remained in motion as I flew headfirst into a sand dune five feet past the tip of my ski.

I sustained massive injuries: shattered pride, ruptured ego, collapsed self-esteem, and hyper-humiliation. Oh, yes, physically, I was unhurt, except for sand ground into my face and a bloody nose—the first symptom I suspect of my deviated septum. As I'm sure you agree, it was all my father's fault. Right?

Not quite. This story shows a classic obstacle in the leader-and-follower relationship: pride. It's different than role confusion. I acknowledged my father was the leader because he had been my teacher, and he was driving the boat. Fine. I needed him to drive, but I didn't need him telling me what to do all the time. I didn't want to be dependent on him, so with pride I declared my independence.

Isn't it interesting that we see the folly of youthful pride so clearly yet overlook the foolishness of spiritual pride? Jesus' disciples certainly missed it. As a result, they stumbled on this major obstacle that keeps us from becoming better followers of Jesus.

THE GREATEST DISCIPLE

In light of the disciples' obscurity before they began following Jesus and their repeated failures along the way, it's intriguing to discover how many times they argued about which of them was the greatest disciple. Even more fascinating is *when* these arguments took place.

The disciples' first game of "King of Discipleship Hill" occurred soon after Jesus' transfiguration. In Luke 9 we learn that Peter, James, and John had just seen Jesus transfigured in glory on the mountaintop. They had seen Him conversing with Moses and Elijah. They had heard a voice saying, "This is my Son, whom I have chosen; listen to him" (Luke 9:35). Impressive. Memorable. One of those moments that should have provided a sense of perspective on the grand scheme of things. At the same time down below, a father came to the remaining disciples seeking help for his son who was tormented by an evil spirit. The disciples failed, but Jesus healed the boy. Luke tells us that the crowd marveled at what Jesus did. Strange, isn't it, that soon after this, the disciples began arguing: "An argument started among the disciples as to which of them would be the greatest. Jesus, knowing their thoughts, took a little child and had him stand beside him. Then he said to them, 'Whoever welcomes this little child in my name welcomes me; and whoever welcomes me welcomes the one who sent me. For he who is least among you all—he is the greatest'" (Luke 9:46–48).

The disciples heard the lesson but missed the point. As a result, the issue festered and erupted again. This time, the disciples were following Jesus toward Jerusalem. He spoke to them clearly about what awaited Him there: "Now as Jesus was going up to Jerusalem, he took the twelve disciples aside and said to them, 'We are going up to Jerusalem, and the Son of Man will be betrayed to the chief priests and the teachers of the law. They will condemn him to death and will turn him over to the Gentiles to be mocked and flogged and crucified. On the third day he will be raised to life!'" (Matt. 20:17–19).

What a powerful moment. The Son of God had just told them that He was going to die. How would His disciples respond? Not as we would expect. James and John apparently got worried that Jesus was going to die before finalizing the title for "Greatest Disciple." Since time was short, they set aside their personal ambitions and (using their mother as an intermediary) simply asked Jesus to designate them as the "Top Two Disciples." Which brother sat on His right-hand side and which sat on His left didn't really matter, they suggested, just as long as they were both at His side. Notice how the other ten disciples responded to this preemptive strike by James and John: "When the ten heard about this, they were indignant with the two brothers. Jesus called them together and said, 'You know that the rulers of the Gentiles lord it over them, and their high officials exercise authority over them. Not so with you. Instead, whoever wants to become great among you must be your servant, and whoever wants to be first must be your slave—just as the Son of Man did not come to be served, but to serve, and to give his life as a ransom for many'" (Matt. 20:24–28).

Why were the others "indignant"? Because James and John had responded inappropriately? No way! The remaining ten disciples were ticked off because "the Sons of Thunder" had beat them to the punch with Jesus. Even as Jesus taught them again about true greatness, they focused on the "gold medal" they wanted—uncontested status as the official greatest disciple. This issue was not resolved, and the final time it erupted defies comprehension.

It was their last night together, and Jesus planned the evening for maximum emotional and spiritual impact. When they arrived at the room where they would share the Passover meal, Jesus surprised them by taking off His outer garment, wrapping a towel around His waist, pouring water in a basin, and then washing the disciples' feet. The disciples were stunned by Jesus' servant role, so Jesus explained the significance of what He had just done for them:

When he had finished washing their feet, he put on his clothes and returned to his place. "Do you understand what I have done for you?" he asked them. "You call me 'Teacher' and 'Lord,' and rightly so, for that is what I am. Now that I, your Lord and Teacher, have washed your feet, you also should wash one another's feet. I have set you an example that you should do as I have done for you. I tell you the truth, no servant is greater than his master, nor is a messenger greater than the one who sent him. Now that you know these things, you will be blessed if you do them." (John 13:12–17)

Then came the Last Supper—bread and wine, symbols of His body and His blood and a vivid picture of the sacrifice He would make. What thoughts must have gone through the disciples' minds? We know one thought shared by all. An important thought. An unresolved issue: "Also a dispute arose among them as to which of them was considered to be greatest. Jesus said to them, 'The kings of the Gentiles lord it over them; and those who exercise authority over them call themselves Benefactors. But you are not to be like that. Instead, the greatest among you should be like the youngest, and the one who rules like the one who serves. For who is greater, the one who is at the table or the one who serves? Is it not the one who is at the table? But I am among you as one who serves'" (Luke 22:24–27).

Don't miss the significance of what was happening here, for it helps us understand why spiritual pride is such an insidious obstacle in discipleship. The disciples loved Jesus. They were committed to following Him and had sacrificed to do so. But rather than being absorbed by Him, they were absorbed by themselves. Rather than focusing on His obvious greatness, they worried about their comparative greatness. Rather than marveling at what Jesus was about to give, they worried about what they would get. Rather than seeking the end of the line, they elbowed their way to the front. Rather than emulating their Master's service, they jockeyed for position so they would never have to serve each other.

To counteract their irrepressible pride, Jesus urged them to grasp a foundational spiritual fact. As long as they were absorbed with themselves and focused on what they could do on their own, they would miss the potential of true discipleship. Yes, they could become "great disciples," but it was not an exclusive title.

A Model for Greatness

While Jesus' disciples continued to crash into the obstacle of spiritual pride, one of their contemporaries responded in a different way. In contrast to the Twelve, this man had reason to be spiritually prideful. When he arrived on the scene, word spread about his prophetic message and eccentric style like small-town gossip. Crowds flocked to hear him and people began to follow him. In fact, he actually had "disciples" who chose to follow him rather than follow Jesus. But John the Baptist never became fuzzy about his role, and he refused to let others get confused.

When some of his disciples, such as Andrew and John, left him to follow Jesus, he did nothing to stop them. When he saw Jesus pass by, he told the crowd that he was unworthy to untie Jesus' sandals. When Jesus came to him and requested to be baptized, John hesitated because he felt inadequate. Later, as Jesus' ministry expanded and His popularity grew, John's disciples resented the fact that everyone had stopped coming to John and had started going to hear Jesus. John listened but was unfazed by their concern: "To this John replied, 'A man can receive only what is given him from heaven. You yourselves can testify that I said, "I am not the Christ but am sent ahead of him." The bride belongs to the bridegroom. The friend who attends the bridegroom waits and listens for him, and is full of joy when he hears the bridegroom's voice. That joy is mine, and it is now complete. He must become greater; I must become less'" (John 3:27–30).

What an incredible attitude. John knew his role and accepted it. He celebrated his leader: Jesus. He knew that Jesus was the star, not him. As the forerunner, John knew he had an important part to play, and he performed to the best of his ability. But he never worried about whether he was the greatest. He simply said, "He must become greater; I must become less." And so he did. In light of that, listen to what Jesus said about him: "I tell you the truth: Among those born of women there has not risen anyone greater than John the Baptist" (Matt. 11:11).

Not a bad compliment, considering the source. How desperately we need to develop the same attitude John exhibited in his life—an attitude, by the way, that Jesus' disciples ultimately demonstrated as well.

How do we avoid the discipleship obstacle of spiritual pride? Why not do what John did? Our goal should be for Jesus to increase through all we do, all we say, and all we think. With this goal in place, we can let this prayer guide all we do:

Lord, may my thoughts reflect my preoccupation with You and my increasing disinterest in myself. May my words cause others to think more highly of You and never spotlight me. May my actions focus attention on You without prompting praise for what I do. When foolish pride urges me to want more, give me grace to become less so that I may become great in Your eyes.

DISCIPLESHIP WITH YOUR UNIQUE TOUCH

14

People follow in different ways.

Obstacle #3: Comparing Yourself to Other Followers

"A game anyone could play." That's how I envisioned it. As a result, I didn't consider the degree to which the teenagers would compete with each other. I had all I needed: a six-foot-tall, multicolored canvas "earth ball" positioned in the center of a football field; fifty teenagers in one end zone and fifty teenagers in the opposite end zone; boys and girls, middle and high schoolers divided evenly among the two teams; a whistle blow to signal the two teams to race toward the ball; goal lines for one team or the other to push the giant ball through thereby winning the game.

I was a young youth minister at the time, and this was my first summer camp. On my best days, I knew just enough to be dangerous. What my mind could conceive, I readily inflicted on my youth group. To my credit, I did sense problems developing in this game as soon as I blew the whistle. From the sidelines, I detected subtle factors for which I had not planned and which would lead to unintended consequences.

The high school football players on both teams had lined up in three-point stances and fired off from the line, barreling toward the ball at the fifty-yard line. Quick sideline calculations revealed that they would reach the ball from opposite sides at approximately the same moment. Attempting to join the athletes on both teams were the fast kids, both boys and girls. Although smaller than the athletes, their speed ensured that they would reach the ball at the same time. Running about ten yards behind were the enthusiastic try-real-hards who wanted desperately to be in the game even if they missed the initial impact.

87

A group of battle-wise youth sponsors clustered with me on the sideline. We all could see what was about to happen, yet we were powerless to prevent it. The dam had burst and the raging flow of teenage bodies would meet in the middle.

The football players on Team 1 slammed into the earth ball approximately 3.78 milliseconds before Team 2 with an impact that supplied the initial force that set the earth ball in motion—an action searching for a reaction. It didn't have to look far.

The Team 2 football players along with their fleet-footed try-real-hards were inches away from the opposite side of the earth ball at the time of Team 1 impact. As a result, their bodies became the first counterforces that reacted to the ball and sent a shock wave of energy back toward Team 1.

The resulting chain reaction was impressive. Atoms split, and energy exploded. First-impact players from both teams bounced in spectacular fashion in opposite directions, driven not by the ball, but rather by the force transmitted through the ball from opposite sides. Their experience was similar to racing full speed into a vertical trampoline. As the ball rocketed through Team 2, it flattened those immediately behind the football players, then mowed down a group of middle school girls. As it rolled, the rough canvas ball scraped skin from chins, noses, and foreheads before stopping down field.

Once it became clear that the injuries were minor (if you include the try-real-hard with the dislocated shoulder in the "minor" category) and that no lawsuits were forthcoming, I paused to reflect on my earth ball experience. My game had one fatal flaw: everyone tried to play like the football players, but most of the teenagers were ill-prepared for the role. The results were disastrous because people didn't play the game in a way that maximized their unique strengths. And of course, their leader did nothing to help them. What a fiasco!

ADAPTING TO THE FOLLOWERS

Sometimes we treat discipleship like that ill-conceived game of earth ball and view following Jesus as a competitive activity in which we observe other Christians and assess our performance against what they do or fail to do. By focusing on them, we seek to determine if we are performing adequately. What we miss, though, is that while Jesus invites everyone to follow Him, He extends a unique invitation to every person. We all get to follow Jesus, but we do not follow Him the same way or with the same results.

We've already seen that role confusion is the most significant obstacle in discipleship. If we begin to act as if we are leaders rather than followers, the entire discipleship process grinds to a halt. The second obstacle, spiritual pride, is equally insidious. If we become self-absorbed and strive to increase our own status because we are following Jesus, discipleship becomes a shallow sham. But the third obstacle is equally destructive—comparing ourselves with other followers. In fact, it reminds me of the story about the three hikers on a mountain trail. One hundred yards away, they saw a huge grizzly bear lumbering their way. Two of the men said, "Let's get out of here." But the third stopped to tie his shoes. The first two called, "What are you doing? If you don't hurry, you'll never outrun that bear." The third man yelled, "I don't have to outrun that bear; I just have to outrun you."

One Game but Many Players

Fortunately, Jesus did not design discipleship as a competitive event in which we scout our opponents to determine their strengths and weaknesses so we can gain an advantage over them. By looking at the people Jesus chose as His first followers, we know He valued diversity. His disciples were a grab bag of mixed abilities and potential, yet in each of them Jesus saw strengths needed in the Kingdom's work. His plan was for them to complement each other, not compete with each other. Nonetheless, His initial choice of future leaders must have left people scratching their heads in bewilderment. Nothing about the apostles stood out; in fact, one-fourth of the group were almost invisible.

The Invisible Four

Aside from being mentioned in the biblical listing of apostles, we hear nothing more about Bartholomew, Simon (the Zealot), or James (son of Alphaeus). They were "with Jesus" but did nothing spectacular or notorious. Thaddaeus (also called Judas, son of James) is mentioned only once, and even his one reference was used to differentiate him from Judas, the traitor: "Then Judas (not Judas Iscariot) said, 'But, Lord, why do you intend to show yourself to us and not to the world?'" (John 14:22).

So, of the twelve Jesus called, one-fourth never merited another mention in the scriptural record. For a group of followers destined to change the world, that was a less-than-impressive beginning. Yet what a comfort for us today. From the beginning, Jesus affirmed that there is a place in discipleship for behind-the-scenes folks, just-get-the-job-done men and women. The silent four disciples remind us that over the long haul, ordinary people make great contributions to the work of the Kingdom as they follow Jesus in their own quiet way.

God-Sensitive Helpers

Philip and Andrew distinguished themselves through their intense desire to know God and their willingness to serve. When they first heard about Jesus, they followed Him, believing that Jesus was "The Hope" that John the Baptist had proclaimed. Later, Philip's statement captured the spiritual passion that he and Andrew shared: "Philip said, 'Lord, show us the Father and that will be enough for us'" (John 14:8).

Discipleship is passionate, and these men channeled the energy of their lives into following Jesus and helping others do the same. Andrew told Simon Peter about Jesus; Philip told Nathanael. Later, they teamed up to bring a boy's sack lunch to Jesus, who multiplied it to feed more than five thousand people. On another occasion, they brought a group of Greek "seekers" directly to Jesus, thereby demonstrating their affinity with anyone of any race who earnestly sought God.

Philip and Andrew weren't "spotlight" people like some of the other disciples. They were not in Jesus' inner circle. They were often excluded from the most spectacular spiritual experiences. Yet they continued to love and serve Jesus. They didn't seek recognition; they simply wanted to be with Jesus and help others find Him also. By choosing them, Jesus affirmed the value of their spiritually sensitive discipleship.

A Dark Past and a Great Heart

Matthew, always tagged as "the tax collector," remained relatively obscure in the scriptural record. The only time his light blazed was immediately after he became a disciple and gave a party to introduce his friends to Jesus: "While Jesus was having dinner at Matthew's house, many tax collectors and 'sinners' came and ate with him and his disciples. When the Pharisees saw this, they asked his disciples, 'Why does your teacher eat with tax collectors and "sinners"?' On hearing this, Jesus said, 'It is not the healthy who need a doctor, but the sick. But go and learn what this means: "I desire mercy, not sacrifice." For I have not come to call the righteous, but sinners'" (Matt. 9:10–13).

Whenever critics wanted to blast Jesus with a serious accusation, they noted that He spent time with "tax collectors and sinners." Surely they had Matthew in mind. Perhaps he became the "conscience" for the other apostles who tended toward exclusion rather than inclusion. Because he knew what it was like to be a spiritual "outsider," he never forgot the grace that made him a spiritual "insider" and gave him the opportunity to follow Jesus. Yes, Matthew had a dark past, but grace gave him a tender heart. By including Matthew, Jesus affirmed that anyone can follow Him and that the past can provide a foundation for effective future ministry.

A Man of Thoughtful Passion

Although Thomas became famous for his doubts, the few references to him in Scripture focus on his strong commitment to Jesus. He was an all-or-nothing guy, willing to commit everything for a cause in which he believed. His passion showed as Jesus led the apostles on their final walk toward Jerusalem: "Then Thomas (called Didymus) said to the rest of the disciples, 'Let us also go, that we may die with him'" (John 11:16).

Yet Thomas was an analytical person, a serious thinker whose heart could not accept what his mind rejected. So when Jesus began talking about the future—where He was going and what the apostles would do—Thomas voiced his confusion: "Thomas said to him, 'Lord, we don't know where you are going, so how can we know the way?'" (John 14:5).

After Jesus' death, and despite the testimony of other disciples, Thomas could not believe that Jesus had risen from the dead. Only a personal meeting with Jesus could settle his doubts and seal his commitment: "A week later His disciples were in the house again, and Thomas was with them. Though the doors were locked, Jesus came and stood among them and said, 'Peace be with you!' Then he said to

Thomas, 'Put your finger here; see my hands. Reach out your hand and put it into my side. Stop doubting and believe.' Thomas said to him, 'My Lord and my God!'" (John 20:26–28).

By choosing Thomas, Jesus affirmed that there is room among His followers for men and women who bring both questions and passion to discipleship. Jesus knew that in time truth satisfies the mind and faith enables hearts to rejoice. Rather than rebuking these types of people for their doubts, Jesus affirmed their potential for great faith. Such an approach to discipleship can become a great gift to others who follow Jesus with fewer questions and untested passion.

The Trio of Thunder and Lightning

Jesus often left the other apostles and spent time alone with James, John, and Peter. Only these three joined Him in the room as Jesus raised Jairus's daughter from the dead. Only they traveled with Him to the Mount of Transfiguration. Only they accompanied Jesus to the inner sanctum of the garden as He prayed the night before His crucifixion.

James and John (nicknamed the "Sons of Thunder") loved Jesus and loved to be with Him. In fact, as we noted earlier, they felt certain that Jesus would want them to sit on His right and left hand in heaven. No one had to coax these men out of their shells. They were strong personalities with leadership potential, and Jesus invested time in them.

If James and John were the "thunder," Simon Peter was the lightning. He required an even greater portion of Jesus' attention. He was an unbroken stallion, powerful and unpredictable. Recognizing his potential for greatness and propensity for failure, Jesus allowed him to sense God's power and face his own weaknesses.

By choosing Peter, James, and John as His inner circle, Jesus demonstrated that identifying spiritual potential is one thing, but harnessing it is another. At times, it appeared their arrogant pride and stubborn self-sufficiency would overwhelm their spiritual potential. But Jesus didn't give up on them, and in time their energy was channeled for Kingdom purposes. Yes, Jesus wants those among us with strong personalities who step naturally into leadership. The good news, though, is that Jesus can transform natural abilities into spiritual capabilities that fill unique roles in the work of the Kingdom.

Unique Expressions of Discipleship

Think of the spectrum of people Jesus chose as His first followers: the Invisible Four; two quiet helpers with sensitive hearts; a sinner with a dark past but a great heart; a man characterized by both enormous passion and great doubts; and a trio of thunder and lightning who would lead people somewhere but not necessarily to the right place. Jesus chose them all and loved them all. Oh yes, there was one more: Judas, the traitor. He, too, was with Jesus during His entire ministry. Apparently, during the early years, even Judas believed he had the potential to be one of Jesus' "great ones." And at the last supper, Jesus expressed love for him in spite of what he was preparing to do.

Yes, all of us bring a confusing set of strengths and weaknesses to discipleship. One day we progress and then do unbelievably foolish things the next. But Jesus never gives up on us. He sees our unique potential and gives us time to develop and grow. That's why comparing ourselves with each other becomes such an obstacle for us in discipleship. Jesus didn't invite us to follow Him *in spite of* who we are. He invited us *because of* who we are. His grace enables Him to love each of us and to see the unique contribution that we can make as we follow Him. All He asks is that we keep our eyes on Him and allow Him to help us become the best followers we can be. We need to learn a lesson I'm trying to teach my younger daughter.

Younger siblings, especially "number two" children, always struggle to find their spot in the family pecking order. The firstborn has already blazed most trails and cashed in much of the family's initial stash of emotion for the "firsts," such as the first birthday party, first Christmas, first lessons, and the first organizational participation. Face it—the second kid must battle for space and attention and the inalienable right to live out from under the firstborn's shadow.

My younger daughter, Kelly, knows this battle well. Three years younger than her sister, Courtney, she is close enough in age to long for inclusion in everything that the "big kids" do but young enough to be chronically excluded. As we have watched her struggle, we have challenged her to be her own person, to quit worrying about what her older sister does and says, and simply do the things she enjoys and in which she excels. Our pep talks have had some effect. Recently, I was in her room and she pointed to her dry-erase board on the wall. On it, she had written:

B.Y.O.P.
Be Your Own Person

I smiled and affirmed her bold declaration and continue to reinforce it. When I observe her doing something on her own, developing a skill or getting involved in a new activity, I say, "Kelly, you're doing a great job on that. You are really becoming your own person. Way to go." She always beams. The battle isn't over, but at least we have surfaced the issue and are working together to help her follow God's path for her.

If we can do that with our family members, how much more does our Heavenly Father want His spiritual children to stop comparing ourselves with others and to find and use the unique gifts and abilities He has placed in our lives. Perhaps God wants us to add a sign in our rooms:

B.Y.O.D.
Be Your Own Disciple

Discipleship is not about competition or comparison; rather, it is about potential. The question is not whether I will be a better disciple than you but whether I will become a better follower of Jesus. Let's get our eyes off of each other and focus on Jesus. It will be more exciting and will help us avoid a major discipleship obstacle. Ready? Be your own disciple!

No
Easy Road

15

Sometimes it's hard to follow

Obstacle #4: Unrealistic Expectations
The chair lift moved slowly up the mountain, and the small, wooden, snow-covered ramp gradually came into view. We watched pairs of skiers ease forward in their seats, position their skis and poles and then slide gracefully down the ramp. How effortless they made the transition from chair lift to ski run. My friend had been right: it was easy. Of course that was before I discovered that my friend was a bold-faced liar.

Relentlessly, the lift carried us toward the ramp. "Anyone can do it," my friend had assured me. Not convinced, I asked, "Even if it's their first time skiing?" "Sure," she replied, "that's the best way to learn. Just ride to the top and learn as you go."

Another pair slid down the ramp with graceful precision, like Olympic ice dancers. Only two more to go. I fidgeted in my seat, noticing that my skies kept crossing at the tips like an X. Intuitively, I sensed that was bad so I struggled to un-X my skis.

The final pair slid down the ramp. "Ease up in the seat," my friend counseled. "Hold your poles in your left hand." I did as instructed. "Ski tips up," the sign on the ramp house ordered. I obeyed.

At the last moment, I observed something hidden from my down-mountain vantage point: the ramp was steep. By then it was too late. Could I simply stay in the chair and ride down the mountain, I wondered? No time. "All right," my friend said, "here we go." Gracefully, she slid out of the chair and down the ramp.

I hesitated. The lift rose as it prepared to descend the mountain and at the last moment, I lunged from my seat. My skis crossed while my forward momentum flung my upper body down the ramp dragging and twisting skis in the air behind me. Ski poles dug into my legs; hard-packed snow cut my face.

The operator sounded the alarm, and the lift screeched to a stop. Everyone on the hill looked at me. Those hanging in suspended lift chairs in the icy wind glared at me. I lay motionless, pinned to the ramp. "Move over to the side," the operator ordered. So I flopped and twisted off the ramp like a wounded armadillo clipped by a car. As I rolled into a snow bank, I heard faint laughter.

That was the high point of my first-day ski experience. The rest of the day was downhill—literally. After struggling to stand on my skis, I discovered the lift was not the only part of skiing my friend had lied about. Tumbling down a mountain the first time you're on skis is *not* the best way to learn. Knowing how to perform minor maneuvers like turning and stopping would have been helpful. Since I lacked every essential skill, my first attempts at skiing had the grace of a deranged moth ramming repeatedly into a lighted bulb: noisy brushes with death followed by disoriented motion in repeated cycles. I learned a valuable lesson that day: If the road ahead is rough, it's better to know it up front. Then your expectations will be realistic. On the other hand, faulty information leads to false expectations, which always result in profound frustration. Unrealistic expectations not only cause problems on the ski slopes, they create major obstacles in discipleship

Nothing but the Truth

In contrast to my *ex*-friend, Jesus told people the truth about discipleship, describing both the challenges as well as the benefits. Although He welcomed all who wanted to follow, Jesus never implied discipleship would be easy. Sometimes, people tagged along with Jesus because they were caught up in the emotion generated by His teaching and miracles. But when these "wannabe" disciples babbled their heartfelt intention to follow Jesus wherever He went, He popped their naive balloons with the pin-prick of truth. For example, Jesus used an illustration of a builder preparing to construct a tower: "Suppose one of you wants to build a tower. Will he not first sit down and estimate the cost to see if he has enough money to complete it? For if he lays the foundation and is not able to finish it, everyone who sees it will ridicule him, saying, 'This fellow began to build and was not able to finish'" (Luke 14:28–30).

The lesson? Don't commit before you calculate; don't start what you cannot finish. Discipleship will be costly, so there is no need to wait for a "blue light special." Jesus offers no "lowest price guarantees" for discipleship, no shop-around-and-compare plans. In fact, Jesus used the image of a king preparing for war to help people adjust their expectations from the beginning: "Or suppose a king is about to go to war against another king. Will he not first sit down and consider whether he is able with ten thousand men to oppose the one coming against him with twenty thousand? If he is not able, he will send a delegation while the other is still a long way off and will ask for terms of peace" (Luke 14:31–32).

True discipleship moves people into the spiritual battle zone, and Jesus wants people who are prepared to join the battle. In reality, though, Jesus never stopped anyone from following Him. He simply helped clarify their expectations so they could make a decision. Without giving them complete details about what was coming, He challenged them to get ready for a rough road but a great journey.

That sort of balanced perspective is what I always admired about my favorite youth sponsor in my church, a woman named Jaly. She worked with teenagers for years and had realistic expectations. Yet she always said yes when I asked her for help. Jaly never knew what kind of "rough road" awaited us on each new trip, but it didn't matter. She would be ready. The rest of us were certainly glad she was with us when that "rough road" included *El Omnibus de Muerte* —The Bus of Death.

UNFAZED BY THE HARD ROAD

Our three buses and van slowed for our second encounter with the Mexican border guards. A week earlier, inspectors had detained our youth choir for several hours until we paid the "unofficial taxes" to the proper official. Now, for the return crossing, we had a plan and two secret weapons: *El Omnibus de Muerte* and Jaly.

El Omnibus de Muerte pulled first into the inspection area. Our other two buses and van stopped behind it. A border guard stepped into the bus. In the front seat, immediately to his left, sat Jaly. She looked up and smiled. The stern-faced man stood by the driver and looked down the trough-like center aisle that separated the double rows of raised seats on either side. Suddenly his face grimaced in disgust and his hand raised to shield his nose. Jaly kept smiling. Hastily, the inspector turned, stepped out of the bus, and signaled for all three buses and the van to cross the border out of Mexico. Just in case you're ever in a similar circumstance, I'll share our top-secret plan so you can use it if necessary.

Initially, Jaly was not the leader on bus 3. She volunteered for duty along with our trip physician, Dr. Don, when a third of our group contracted a vile stomach disorder with the full range of disgusting symptoms. As the plague multiplied, the adult sponsors determined that the afflicted should be isolated on one bus. The healthy teenagers began calling it the Bus of Death. It was a place of torment, the outer darkness filled with wailing and gnashing of teeth—certainly not a place anyone wanted to go. Dr. Don had to go because he was the doctor. And Jaly went, well, because the rest of our sponsors were wimps.

As the plague worsened, Dr. Don moved mercifully through the bus giving the kids "knock-out shots"—injections that calmed their stomachs and made them sleep. As Jaly explained later, that plan worked well until she looked back and saw Dr. Don sitting in a seat, his face contorted and pale, giving himself a shot. Some people have it; some people don't.

The amazing thing was that in spite of her experience on the Bus of Death, Jaly kept volunteering as a youth sponsor. She modeled discipleship in action—discipleship built on realistic expectations of the challenges and the rewards.

A BARGAIN AT ANY PRICE

Jesus knew that in time people would recognize discipleship as a prize of inestimable value and would pay the price required. To drive home this point, He told two stories with the same theme.

The kingdom of heaven is like treasure hidden in a field. When a man found it, he hid it again, and then in his joy went and sold all he had and bought that field. (Matt. 13:44)

Again, the kingdom of heaven is like a merchant looking for fine pearls. When he found one of great value, he went away and sold everything he had and bought it. (Matt. 13:45–46)

In the stories, both men found something of great value—a rare pearl and a treasure in a field. Both went and sold all they had so that they could purchase the treasures. They gave all they had but gained far more in the transaction. In essence, they gave pennies for treasures. In contrast, the Book of Genesis records the story of Esau, who traded his birthright for a pot of stew. He traded a treasure for pennies. As I considered this contrast, I wrote a song called "Pennies for Treasures." The chorus included these lines:

> He is no fool who gives what he can't keep
> To gain what he never can lose.
> You'll give pennies for treasures or treasures for pennies
> It all depends which one you choose.[7]

In one sense, the decision to follow Jesus is hard. As one leader said, "Salvation may be free, but discipleship will cost you everything." Yet in another way, the decision to follow Jesus is easy. As we set aside anything that keeps us from following Jesus with abandon, we exchange our penny-clutching lives for spiritual treasures.

Unfortunately, the consumer mentality that governs our buying decisions today has influenced the way some people evaluate Christianity. As a result, people dabble in Christianity as long as it doesn't cost them anything, or at least not much. Even when shown the price tag for full discipleship, they haggle for a discount. That is not the way of the cross.

Dietrich Bonhoeffer said years ago, "When Christ calls a man, he bids him to come and die." Such words sound ominous in our age of indulgence. Yet those words capture the essence of Jesus' message. Anything less than full-price discipleship cheapens the grace Christ offers and dilutes the answers faith provides. Without holding back, we should follow Christ with robust faith and full commitment so our lives conform with Jesus' succinct call to discipleship: "Then he said to them all: 'If anyone would come after me, he must deny himself and take up his cross daily and follow me'" (Luke 9:23).

In light of Jesus' explanation, we cannot settle for anything less or expect anything easier. We cannot discount that for which Jesus died. For such a prize, no price is too great, and even the ultimate price is a bargain.

16 SPIRITUAL POP TESTS

*Testing while following
enhances learning.*

Obstacle #5: Misunderstanding the Purpose of Testing

On the campus of Baylor University, Professor Robert Reed (Mr. Reed to the students) was a living legend. As a historian, he had enough knowledge to stand toe-to-toe with any academic peer; but he had other qualities that endeared him to many on campus. In fact, many students considered their experience at Baylor incomplete without taking at least one course from this "master teacher." He possessed that rare ability to make history come alive. Plus, his self-effacing manner, warm smile, and quirky sense of humor spawned numerous "Mr. Reed stories." One became a campus favorite and was passed along for years.

As the story goes, one history class began the semester by asking Mr. Reed if he ever gave pop quizzes. He didn't respond. Instead, he walked to the window of his second-floor classroom and stared outside. After a few moments, he turned, walked toward the class with a dismissive smile, and said, "The day I give you a pop quiz will be the day I come in through that window." Everyone laughed, relieved that pop quizzes posed no threat.

Weeks later, class began and Mr. Reed was not there. Students waited, wondering if they would be able to "walk" class. Suddenly, metal clanged against brick outside the classroom and drew everyone's attention to the front of the room. Then Mr. Reed's bald head popped through the open window. He smiled at the astonished class and then leaned through the window while shaking a stack of papers. "Class, get out your pencils," he said. "Here's your pop quiz."

As far as we know, Jesus never climbed through second-floor windows to give discipleship tests; but as *the* master-teacher, He used a variety of tests to help His students learn.

JESUS DISCIPLESHIP TESTS

Jesus worked continually to build His disciples' faith. He wanted them to have absolute confidence in Him and trust Him under every circumstance. Otherwise, the difficult times to come would devastate them. So Jesus taught them, then gave periodic tests to assess their progress. In the early stages of His ministry, the tests He gave were relatively simple, but as time passed His tests became increasingly demanding.

The Daily "Follow Me" Quiz

When Jesus encountered Simon, Andrew, James, and John on the seashore, He performed a miracle and then tested their willingness to respond to His leadership.

> When he had finished speaking, he said to Simon, "Put out into deep water, and let down the nets for a catch." . . . When they had done so, they caught such a large number of fish that their nets began to break. . . . When Simon Peter saw this, he fell at Jesus' knees and said, "Go away from me, Lord; I am a sinful man!" For he and all his companions were astonished at the catch of fish they had taken, and so were James and John, the sons of Zebedee, Simon's partners. Then Jesus said to Simon, "Don't be afraid; from now on you will catch men." So they pulled their boats up on shore, left everything and followed him. (Luke 5:4, 6, 8–11)

After inviting them to become "fishers of men," Jesus simply walked away. That was the test. They could either: (A) stay and fish or (B) follow Jesus. They chose B and aced the first quiz. But as we saw in part 2 of our study, Jesus gave the disciples this test repeatedly. Every day, He moved on, and they had to decide to stay put or keep following. Every time they said yes and filed in behind Jesus, their commitment to His Lordship grew stronger. The daily quizzes proved they were progressing. Yet Jesus had other surprises in store for them.

The Faith Pop Test

One evening, Jesus told His disciples to load up the boat and head across the lake. They had no idea they were about to take a "doozy" of a pop test. A furious squall arose and waves nearly swamped the boat. The disciples, many of whom were experienced fishermen, panicked because of the storm's severity. Terrified and desperate, they sought Jesus' help. To their utter astonishment, they found Him asleep: "Jesus was in the stern, sleeping on a cushion. The disciples woke him and said to him, 'Teacher, don't you care if we drown?'" (Mark 4:38).

Their question packed a truckload of emotion. The disciples felt frightened, overwhelmed, and confused. Worst of all, they wondered if their leader understood their plight. How could He care for them, they reasoned, if He snoozed while they struggled? Rather than answer their question with words, Jesus answered with action: "He got up, rebuked the wind and said to the waves, 'Quiet! Be still!' Then the wind died down and it was completely calm. He said to his disciples, 'Why are you so afraid? Do you still have no faith?'" (Mark 4:39–40).

Once the crisis passed and the disciples' hearts stopped racing, Jesus gave them a two-part, extra-point bonus question so they could raise their scores on the quiz. For Part One, Jesus asked, "Why are you so afraid?" The disciples probably answered that one quickly. "We were afraid because we thought we were about to die!" Good answer. Most of us would have said the same thing. Yet Part Two of the question probed the real issue. "Do you still have no faith?" That one was tougher to answer. Suddenly, the experience they had just endured took on new significance—spiritual significance.

By stilling the storm, Jesus demonstrated that He had ample power to protect them in a life-threatening situation. There was no reason for fear, unless, of course, they questioned either His power or His concern or both. Instantly, Jesus' bonus question shifted the focus from the storm at sea to the storm of faith that raged in their hearts.

In reality, sea storms were far less threatening than heart storms. Jesus could calm sea storms with a single command. Heart storms, however, would continue until the disciples developed full confidence in His power and His concern. The disciples would only gain that kind of confidence after repeated encounters with His faithfulness. Further testing was certainly required.

The Mission Trip Field Test

Another significant test came when Jesus sent the Twelve to do the things they had seen Him do. By any measure, this was a challenging real-world test that would push them to their limits. "These twelve Jesus sent out with the following instructions: 'Do not go among the Gentiles or enter any town of the Samaritans. Go rather to the lost sheep of Israel. As you go, preach this message: "The kingdom of heaven is near." Heal the sick, raise the dead, cleanse those who have leprosy, drive out demons. Freely you have received, freely give. Do not take along any gold or silver or copper in your belts; take no bag for the journey, or extra tunic, or sandals or a staff; for the worker is worth his keep'" (Matt. 10:5–10).

The Bible doesn't give us a complete assessment of how the disciples did in each of the test categories: healing the sick, raising the dead, cleansing the lepers, and driving out demons. We do know, however, that when they returned, they were thrilled by what they had experienced. Apparently, they achieved some level of success—an amazing feat considering the assignment. In part, the test may have gauged their willingness to do as told. On either scale—willingness to go or actual results—they passed. This did not, however, complete the testing. In fact, the most difficult test was yet to come.

The Final Exam
On the trip to Jerusalem, the disciples sensed the gravity of the situation. Increasingly, Jesus shared openly about what was going to happen to Him and to them. On one level, they were ready to face it. Years of following Jesus coupled with quizzes, pop tests, and field tests had given them confidence in their spiritual development. Thomas even declared his willingness to die for Jesus—the ultimate test for any follower. The other disciples joined him in this bold declaration.

Things changed quickly when events escalated with shocking intensity. As the soldiers arrested Jesus in the garden of Gethsemane, His disciples finally faced the ultimate test. When suffering and death stood before them, they turned in their examination booklets and ran from class. Of course, none of this surprised Jesus; He had warned them. Before the final, they had been so cocky, confident they could handle whatever happened. As a result, when they deserted Jesus, they also gave up on themselves. They assumed they had flunked the course. Fortunately for them (and for us!), Jesus did not give up on them. Like all the other tests, the "final" was not the end. It was simply one more chance to mark progress and indicate room for growth. Jesus was not finished with them yet. Like many of us, though, the disciples had not learned to welcome their tests.

GOD'S PURPOSE FOR TESTING

Ask most children why teachers give tests and their answers will range from "because they are mean" to "they just want to see what we don't know." This is what I thought, especially in the third grade. I was convinced that Mrs. Smith gave spelling tests to ruin my life.

Her standards were high—100 percent correct—if you wanted to have a paper railroad car with your name on it displayed in the class "Spelling Train." The students who spelled all the words correctly could keep their railroad car in the long line thumb-tacked above the blackboard. But those who misspelled words (even one) had to take down their railroad car plus take their spelling paper home and have their parents sign it. My car was not a regular member of the Spelling Train, and I took home plenty of papers for signatures. But not the one with the big, red "65" written across the top. Missing a word wasn't a major problem at my house; but I figured a "65" would push the limits, so I worked out a solution to help my parents avoid an awkward situation. I was so confident about my solution that I wasn't even concerned when Mrs. Smith asked me to come with her to see Mr. Thomason, the principal.

Things took a nasty downward turn when we entered his office. He looked at me for a moment and then said, "John, did your mother sign this paper?" He was holding my spelling paper with my mother's name written at the bottom—in my best third-grade, just-learning-to-do-cursive handwriting.

Looking back, it would have been better if I had played it cool; you know, swaggered and said, "What's the matter? Can't read cursive yet?" That would have had impact. Instead, I started crying—always a dead giveaway. Crying was, however, what stopped Mr. Thomason from calling my parents. Both he and Mrs. Smith were so moved by my display of remorse that they decided the worst punishment would be for me to take my paper home, explain to my parents why I had forged my mother's name, and then get the paper signed. Talk about corporal punishment!

In spite of my dire circumstances, I still didn't learn my lesson. As I saw it, both my teacher and the principal had ganged up to destroy my life with spelling tests. They could have explained that the tests were designed to help me learn, to build my character, and to ensure I had a better life. I would not have believed them. At that moment, my focus was decidedly short-term.

I'm embarrassed to say that in addition to forging my mother's name initially, I made another poor choice, one that I have not revealed either orally or in print to this point because I've worried about the negative influence it may have on children. (Plus I've never told my parents.) But since few children are going to read this book, I'm ready to tell all.

I never showed that paper to my parents. I got a copy of my father's signature, traced it on my spelling paper, turned my "signed" paper in the next day, and never heard another word about it. As it turned out, although I couldn't spell and couldn't forge, I could trace. Of course, weaseling out of that situation hindered my character development and nurtured a bent toward deviousness for which I paid in the years to come. I discovered that if we resist life's tests, we simply have to take them again later.

Teachers give tests to reveal what we know, not to uncover what we don't know. Tests indicate areas of strength we can celebrate and point out areas of weakness that need additional attention. They reflect both the quality of the learning and the quality of the teaching. Tests are really wonderful, but it took me years to understand that reality in my education, and even longer to learn that the same truths apply in discipleship.

God's Personalized Testing Program
Unlike our teachers, God knows exactly what we have mastered and what we still need to learn in discipleship. Consequently His tests are for our benefit only. That is why He allows situations in our lives that reveal our spiritual progress as well as our need for continued growth. Without tests, we can become discouraged, unsure if we have developed more of Christ's character or moved further in our spiritual journey. On the other hand, without tests, we can become cocky, convincing ourselves we are mature followers when in fact we lack basic skills and essential values.

God tests us for our good. Perhaps you have experienced some of the following tests. If not, get ready. Test time will come.

Will you follow? Sometimes God draws us into a new situation so we must decide again if we will follow as He directs or stay where we are.

Why are you following? God puts us in situations that reveal our true motivation for following Jesus. If we discover we are seeking only what we can gain through discipleship, we will have the opportunity to repent and develop new values.

Are you a happy follower? God often tests our attitudes as well as our obedience. Not only does God want us to follow, but to follow joyfully. He often allows challenging circumstances and difficult people in our lives so we can gauge our capacity to follow Him without complaining and whining.

Will you follow alone? God sometimes places us in situations in which we must follow Him in a direction that is not popular. As others move the opposite way, we quickly learn if we are willing to follow as He leads while enduring the criticism of other people.

Will you follow when the way is hard? Sometimes, God allows us to travel through difficult situations and painful experiences. In those settings, we discover if we are willing to follow Him when everything within us wants to turn and run.

Will you follow when it costs you everything? God has every right to lead us into circumstances in which following Him may cost us our physical lives. Only through His grace in that moment could any of us endure. But we must never forget that the records of Christian history are filled with stories of ordinary people who faced and passed this ultimate test.

Rather than resisting the tests God brings to our lives, we should welcome them. Every test helps us learn, revealing more about us and more about God's faithfulness. Testing is an integral part of discipleship. If we accept that fact and let God teach us what we need to know, we can avoid a major obstacle in discipleship.

Repeat after me: Tests are good. Tests are good. Tests are good.

THE NEXT STEP
BEYOND FAILURE

*Those who fail
can follow again.*

Obstacle #6: Failure

Charles Ponzi came up with a great scheme. Over the years, so many hucksters have adapted his basic scam that it has become his legacy. A Ponzi Scheme.

Here's how it works. The con artist offers extraordinary rates of return on an investment. As gullible people entrust their money, the con artist pays them the agreed upon interest. Sensing they have found an investor's dream-come-true, the early suckers tell their friends, who invest even more money. As the incoming funds multiply, the con artist pays the early investors using money supplied by the later investors. Of course, all along the way, the huckster skims as much cash as possible for himself. The process obviously cannot continue forever, so eventually there are insufficient funds to pay the required interest payments. The early investors get worried and demand their principal. Rumors spread that the investment is shaky. New money dries up, and soon the entire house of cards falls. The investors lose their money, and the huckster skips the country or goes to jail.

On these matters I speak (unfortunately) with experience. In the early eighties, a modern-day Ponzi set up a fake company that supposedly extracted silver from used film and made astounding profits. This enabled the company to pay their "investors" monthly interest payments of 10 percent or more. Not bad! It sounded too good to be true—and of course it was.

When I explained the opportunity to my wife, she felt uneasy about it but deferred to my judgment (a big mistake). As a result, I invested and ultimately lost several thousand dollars. When the scam became public, it was big news in Garland, Texas. Criminal investigators discovered that the lady who ran the operation had bilked hundreds of people out of millions of dollars. I was, as I later learned, one of the small fish in this deep fat fryer. Ultimately, the lady went to jail, but we "investors" lost our money.

I remember vividly the night I told Lynn Marie what had happened. She could have ranted and raved about my stupidity, but she didn't. She could have reminded me that she had felt uneasy from the beginning, but she kept that historical fact to herself. She could have made me feel even worse about losing money we needed, but she graciously refrained. Obviously, she felt angry and disappointed. But in spite of all that, from then until now, she has never focused on the money I lost. I appreciate many things about Lynn Marie, but the way she responded to this failure in my life stands as a high-water mark of grace. She continued to love me. She gave me hope for the future. And she even let me write checks occasionally.

In Spite of Failure

All of Jesus' followers failed. None, however, failed more frequently or dramatically than Simon Peter. Yet his failures became the foundation on which Jesus built Peter's future as a spiritual leader. This is great news for all of us who want to become better followers of Jesus, because all of us experience times of failure. If we do not understand how Jesus views our failures, they can become major obstacles for us in discipleship. Peter's experiences can change our perspective.

Almost Walking on Water
No one ever accused Peter of thinking before acting. His famous walk-on-water experience stands as a monument to Peter's knack for getting in over his head.

> During the fourth watch of the night Jesus went out to them, walking on the lake. When the disciples saw him walking on the lake, they were terrified. "It's a ghost," they said, and cried out in fear. But Jesus immediately said to them: "Take courage! It is I. Don't be afraid." "Lord, if it's you," Peter replied, "tell me to come to you on the water."

"Come," he said. Then Peter got down out of the boat, walked on the water and came toward Jesus. But when he saw the wind, he was afraid and, beginning to sink, cried out, "Lord, save me!" Immediately Jesus reached out his hand and caught him. "You of little faith," he said, "why did you doubt?" And when they climbed into the boat, the wind died down. (Matt. 14:25–32)

All right, let's be fair and give Peter credit where credit is due. He stepped out of the boat. How far he walked, we don't know. But who cares? He walked on water, and that's impressive. So in what sense did Peter fail? Jesus rebuked Peter for his doubts and his lack of faith. After the first few soggy steps, Peter focused on the waves, lost his nerve, and sank.

With Peter, all this was part of a larger pattern that concerned Jesus. Peter tended to overstate and overreact. No matter what situation he was in or who he was with, Peter believed he was the "big dog." In his eyes, others were pups hiding under the porch. So that night while the other disciples quaked in fear, terrified by the storm and "the ghost" they saw walking toward them, Peter reminded them of their lowly positions once again by asking permission to walk on the water. Jesus must have grinned as He granted that request, knowing it would be a wonderful lesson for Peter on pride, impulsiveness, and erratic faith.

I wish the Bible told us more about what happened. How far did Peter walk? How fast did he sink? How far did he go under water? To his knees? Perhaps to the waist? Possibly to his chin? We don't know for sure, but I suspect Jesus let Peter sink far enough to get his attention before he rescued him. Undoubtedly, it was a lesson in failure Peter never forgot, even though he would need a few more review sessions to drive the truth home.

Speaking for Both Sides

Occasionally, Peter spoke words so rich in spiritual insight that only God could have revealed them. Peter's problem was that he didn't know when to let well enough alone.

His supremely insightful statement came the day Jesus asked what people were saying about Him. The disciples' exit polls with the crowds yielded disappointing and confusing results. Some thought He was John the Baptist; others guessed Elijah. Still others believed He was Jeremiah or one of the prophets. In reality, Jesus was most interested in the disciples' perspective. So with His next question, He shifted the spotlight directly onto them: "'But what about you?' he asked. 'Who do you say I am?'" (Matt. 16:15).

Have you watched elementary school children respond when they believe they know the answer to a question asked in class? Hands wave; small bodies squirm. That's the way I picture Peter responding to Jesus' question. He was positive he knew the right answer and wanted everyone to know it! "Simon Peter answered, 'You are the Christ, the Son of the living God'" (Matt. 16:16).

Jesus couldn't conceal His delight at Peter's response and offered His highest affirmation: "Jesus replied, 'Blessed are you, Simon son of Jonah, for this was not revealed to you by man, but by my Father in heaven. And I tell you that you are Peter, and on this rock I will build my church, and the gates of Hades will not overcome it'" (Matt. 16:17–18).

For Peter, who had the modesty of a peacock, Jesus' affirmation caused his ego to swell to dangerous levels. Without question, it was his moment of glory, a spectacular accomplishment. Perhaps Peter was thinking, *Well, that should settle the argument once and for all about which disciple is the greatest!* Yet Peter was troubled by what Jesus said next. For the first time, Jesus began to describe in detail His forthcoming death. His comments were so shocking that Peter felt obligated to pull Jesus aside and offer a bit of advice: "Peter took him aside and began to rebuke him. 'Never, Lord!' he said. 'This shall never happen to you!'" (Matt. 16:22).

Notice that Peter asked Jesus to step aside for a moment. Apparently, he believed Jesus' remarks were so far off base that he felt awkward correcting Jesus in front of the other disciples. For such a sensitive matter, Jesus needed a private session with His one-and-only source of spiritual truth—Peter. I suspect that Peter anticipated Jesus thanking him warmly for getting His divine plan back on course. Jesus' comments must have sent Peter reeling: "Jesus turned and said to Peter, 'Get behind me, Satan! You are a stumbling block to me; you do not have in mind the things of God, but the things of men'" (Matt. 16:23).

Talk about being whipsawed! Peter flipped from speaking words from the Father in heaven to speaking the words of Satan. What a failure. Yet as Jesus had displayed before, He didn't allow Peter's failure to impede his progress. Jesus knew it was imperative that Peter learn to recognize the voice of the enemy who worked to undermine their mission. But on that day, Peter learned far more about himself. His experience confirmed that he certainly had great potential, both for good and for evil. Unfortunately, this was far from Peter's final failure.

Sleeping Instead of Praying

Rarely did Jesus express His personal needs, and only once did He ask the disciples for personal help. The night before His crucifixion, Jesus' burden grew heavier than He could carry alone. He needed friends with Him, supporting Him, praying for Him. So the Son of God asked for help: "Then Jesus went with his disciples to a place called Gethsemane, and he said to them, 'Sit here while I go over there and pray.' He took Peter and the two sons of Zebedee along with him, and he began to be sorrowful and troubled. Then he said to them, 'My soul is overwhelmed with sorrow to the point of death. Stay here and keep watch with me'" (Matt. 26:36–38).

After all Jesus had done for them, He asked for so little—keep watch and pray. But even the little He asked was too much. "Then he returned to his disciples and found them sleeping. 'Could you men not keep watch with me for one hour?' he asked Peter. 'Watch and pray so that you will not fall into temptation. The spirit is willing, but the body is weak'" (Matt. 26:40–41).

Three times Jesus asked Peter and the others to stay awake and pray for Him. Three times He returned and found them sleeping. Finally it was too late. Judas, accompanied by soldiers, betrayed Jesus, and the time of torture began.

For Peter, failures began to fall in a line like dominoes. Rather than pray, he slept. Rather than fight, he fled. Rather than claim His Lord, he cursed.

Forgetting Your First Love

Peter's final failure was the greatest—the one everyone would remember and that Peter would never forget. Jesus had warned him about what was going to happen, but Peter would not listen: "'Simon, Simon,

Satan has asked to sift you as wheat. But I have prayed for you, Simon, that your faith may not fail. And when you have turned back, strengthen your brothers.' But he replied, 'Lord, I am ready to go with you to prison and to death.' Jesus answered, 'I tell you, Peter, before the rooster crows today, you will deny three times that you know me'" (Luke 22:31–34).

During their last meal, Peter had vehemently declared that he would never deny Jesus. Yet in the end he did—three times. Punctuated with curses for emphasis. "About an hour later another asserted, 'Certainly this fellow was with him, for he is a Galilean.' Peter replied, 'Man, I don't know what you're talking about!' Just as he was speaking, the rooster crowed. The Lord turned and looked straight at Peter. Then Peter remembered the word the Lord had spoken to him: 'Before the rooster crows today, you will disown me three times.' And he went outside and wept bitterly" (Luke 22:59–62).

How ironic that Jesus would be there at that precise moment. Yet I'm convinced that as Jesus looked at Peter, His face showed only disappointment and love. Jesus knew that soon He would talk with Peter about that night of failure. Soon He would extend a new invitation to discipleship. Jesus knew Peter would follow again and follow faithfully until he died a martyr's death. Jesus knew these things; Peter didn't. So as Peter cursed the final time and then saw Jesus looking at him, he crumbled. The isolated hours that followed became the crucible that burned away pride from his life, melting away self-sufficiency and arrogance. All that remained was a warm heart waiting for another chance.

Turning the Corner on Failure

After the resurrection, Jesus appeared one morning to Peter and the other disciples on a beach. It must have reminded Peter of another morning on a similar beach years before, the first time Jesus invited him to follow and become a "fisher of men." Once again, Jesus and Peter had serious spiritual business to complete.

Three times Jesus asked Peter a simple question: "Do you love Me?"

Three times Peter responded, "Lord, You know I love You."

Three times Jesus confronted Peter's worst failure.

Three times Peter held his broken heart before his Lord.

The question was unspoken: "What comes after failure?"

The answer was simple: "The next step."

Jesus foreshadowed the future Peter would experience—a future that held both promise and pain. Just then, Peter saw one of the other disciples walking behind them, so he asked, "What about him?" Jesus cut to the heart of the matter with this statement: "If I want him to remain alive until I return, what is that to you? You must follow me" (John 21:22).

What amazing words: "You must follow me." Words that brought the cycle of discipleship full circle to where it began on a sunlit beach years before. For Peter, discipleship began when Jesus invited him to follow. Fortunately, after failure Jesus simply renewed the invitation.

THE GOOD NEWS ABOUT FAILURE

Failure is a serious but not insurmountable obstacle in discipleship. We all fail, so we all identify with Peter's failures and marvel that Jesus never gave up on him. Like Peter, we sin. We turn our backs on God. Our faith falters. But just as Jesus did with Peter, He forgives us and offers us a future. What comes after failure? One more step. The next step following Jesus. The adventure of discipleship continues.

IV

FOLLOWING A LEADER YOU CANNOT SEE

Followism 18:   You can follow the leader without seeing the leader.

Followism 19:   You can follow the leader by following the leader's written directions.

Followism 20:   You can follow the leader by listening to the leader's voice.

Followism 21:   The better you know the leader, the easier it is to follow.

Followism 22:   When it's dark, stand still and trust the leader.

Moving Up to First-Class Following

18

*You can follow the leader
without seeing the leader.*

In the early 1970s, a fad swept America that changed the nature of following forever: the citizens band radio—CB for short. Before that time, if you wanted to follow another driver to a destination, you had to see that driver. Not so after millions of cars sprouted antennas from their trunks. After that, people could follow drivers who were miles ahead of them. The airwaves became filled with frantic appeals for "breaker 1-9." Millions of drivers "put their ears on," made up silly-sounding "handles" (I was the Guitar Man), and began speaking in unknown tongues about "double nickels," "smoky bears," and "stopping for a 40." No longer did interstate drivers travel alone; everyone wanted to be part of a "convoy."

Before the fad, the "CB Zone" was a strange dimension of time and space inhabited primarily by truckers in their "eighteen-wheelers." For uninitiated "four-wheeler" drivers, early experiences in the CB Zone were enticing but intimidating. Those who bought the equipment first, learned the lingo, and mastered this brave new world of communication amazed the rest of us.

Mike, my college roommate, was the CB guru among my circle of friends. He grew up in Henrietta, Texas—a small, west Texas town with cattle ranches and oil rigs. Mike's family had CBs in every vehicle and a base station in their home—a super-powerful CB that broadcast a signal rivaled only by the voice of God. For us, Mike spoke with absolute authority about life in the CB Zone.

One winter, five carloads of us from Baylor University planned a ski trip to Colorado. Mike left early so he could stop in Henrietta. The rest planned to travel in a CB convoy from Waco and meet him there.

No problem, at least not until Mike decided to guide us from the interstate to his parents' home using his CB base station. Because he was totally confident his plan would work, he gave us no written directions and simply told us to contact him over the radio when we neared Henrietta. Since we were still flushed with CB excitement, we agreed.

About thirty miles out of Henrietta, our convoy attempted to contact Mike on the CB. Only then did we discover that although this new technology made it possible to follow in new ways, a few glitches remained that caused major problems.

> ▶ *Limited power to transmit.* The CBs in our cars were less than state-of-the-art. Only two tin cans with a string tied between them transmitted with less power than our radios.

> ▶ *Vulnerability to interference.* We discovered that in the CB Zone, power corrupts and absolute power corrupts absolutely. At the moment we began our attempts to contact Mike, two truckers with powerful radios settled in for an extended chat. Although we never saw them, their colorful, nonstop conversation overwhelmed our feeble attempts to "break 1-9."

> ▶ *Limited capacity to receive transmissions.* Even though Mike's base station was powerful, our puny mobile CBs couldn't pick up his signal. We tried to reach him, and he tried to reach us; but we failed to connect.

After more than an hour of frustration, the fog of static and gibberish suddenly vanished and we heard Mike's welcome voice. The connection was clear. The signal was strong. He gave us directions, and we moved effortlessly to his parents' home. A breakthrough in CB communication? No, a quarter in a pay phone outside of Henrietta. When we became frustrated with the new technology, we reverted back to the familiar. Our experience convinced us, in fact, that the CB Zone was a hostile environment. When we left Henrietta later that night, we had plenty of maps and kept our leader in sight. As we traveled, we experimented with the CBs, but after wasting so much time earlier, we remained leery. Certainly, CB communication was different, but was it better? We were not convinced.

Hints about a New Plan

When Jesus first told His disciples that He had a new and better way for them to follow, they were not convinced either. In fact, they had no idea what Jesus was talking about and quickly decided that whatever Jesus had in mind would be a step back rather than a step forward. Besides, they liked the way they currently followed Jesus and wanted things to stay the same.

In spite of their mistakes up to that point, they had progressed in their ability to follow Jesus. When He moved on, they packed up and followed. When He chose peculiar routes or gave strange directions, they obeyed. Even when Jesus set His face toward Jerusalem to face His final ordeal, they pledged to stay with Him to the end.

The disciples assumed that following Jesus physically was the only way to follow. Although it was challenging at times, physical following was an objective process. They kept Jesus in sight and stayed with Him. The possibility of following Jesus some other way vapor-locked their minds with confusion. There was nothing subtle about the approach Jesus took with them. He simply dropped the big bomb: that He was going away, that they could not come, but that it was going to be good for them. "But I tell you the truth: It is for your good that I am going away. Unless I go away, the Counselor will not come to you; but if I go, I will send him to you. When he comes, he will convict the world of guilt in regard to sin and righteousness and judgment: in regard to sin, because men do not believe in me; in regard to righteousness, because I am going to the Father, where you can see me no longer" (John 16:7–10).

Put yourself in their shoes. Can you imagine their questions? How could it be good for them if Jesus went away? What could ever replace His physical presence in their lives? How could they possibly follow Him if they could no longer see Him? Jesus, anticipating their questions, continued His explanation. "I have much more to say to you, more than you can now bear. But when he, the Spirit of truth, comes, he will guide you into all truth" (John 16:12–13).

Jesus' words shocked the disciples. They struggled to understand who this "Spirit of truth" was and how He could possibly enable them to follow Jesus in the future. They cringed at the thought of being separated from Jesus.

"All this I have spoken while still with you. But the Counselor, the Holy Spirit, whom the Father will send in my name, will teach you all things and will remind you of everything I have said to you" (John 14:25–26). Jesus made the future sound so simple. In essence, He described two phases of following. In Phase One, the disciples had followed Jesus physically. In Phase Two, they would follow Him spiritually. In Phase One, they followed a leader they could see. In Phase Two, they would follow a leader they could not see. In both phases, they would follow Him, but the new "following" would maintain the best elements of the past while adding some incredible enhancements. The disciples were not convinced. From their perspective, there was nothing wrong with physically following Jesus. It was working. Why foul up a good thing?

THE NEW AND IMPROVED MODEL

Jesus knew the disciples were trapped in a Phase One Following mindset. This blinded them to the restrictions of their current approach and the potential of a new type of "following" relationship. Consider these Phase One problems and how Jesus proposed to solve them with Phase Two solutions.

Problems and Solutions

Now you're with Me; now you're not. The disciples enjoyed being with Jesus. But that experience limited both what He and they could do. Their lives orbited around Him. They went where He went. What they really needed, however, was a way to follow Jesus without being fettered by physical restrictions. Under Phase Two Following, the disciples could be with Jesus continually.

Now I say it; then you learn it. While the disciples were with Jesus, they were learning; yet if they were not with Jesus, they stopped learning. What they really needed was a way to learn spiritual truth continually. Under Phase Two Following, the Holy Spirit would communicate truth and update spiritual insights that grew out of their continual relationship with Jesus.

First you know it; then you forget it. Jesus' disciples heard more spiritual truth than they could absorb. As a result, Jesus spent an enormous amount of time rehashing old lessons. The disciples needed a way to recall spiritual truths when they most needed them. Under Phase Two Following, the Holy Spirit would teach them and then help them apply that truth during their times of greatest need.

When Jesus spoke initially of a new type of following, the disciples assumed they would get a "less-than" rather than a "more-than" experience. They could not conceive of a way Jesus could give them more of Himself than what He had done during the years they had followed Him physically. But that's exactly what Jesus intended to do. But before the disciples could have more, their old way of following had to end. Certainly, there would be pain in the transition. Yes, it was understandable that the disciples would cling to what they knew rather than embrace what could be. Yet Jesus was the leader, and He gave them no option.

Truth We Struggle to Believe

Many of us struggle to believe that Phase Two Following is better than Phase One Following. If we had the option, we still wish we could follow Jesus physically just like the first disciples. We know Jesus said, "It is good for you that I go away," but we quietly file that statement (with due respect) under "Stuff Jesus Said but Couldn't Possibly Mean." For us, Phase Two Following still sounds like a consolation prize.

Intellectually, we can affirm that it is possible to follow a leader we cannot see. In the physical realm, the relatively primitive communication offered by the CB radio demonstrates this reality. Yet when we think of following Jesus today, we're tempted to use the CB radio metaphor to set our spiritual expectations. Nagging doubts haunt us as we consider our limitations.

Limited capacity to communicate with Jesus. We wonder if we can have a real relationship with Jesus if we can't see Him and cannot be with Him physically. At times, we question if we have the spiritual equipment required to connect us to Jesus.

Inability to overcome interference. Can our feeble spiritual systems overcome spiritual static so that we can communicate with God? While we may suspect some super-transmitting Christians can crank up the power and break through to God, we wonder if we garden-variety Christians can do the same thing.

Limited capacity to receive transmissions. Even with our spiritual antennas cranked to maximum height, we still wonder if God's signal can reach us. When we fail to hear from God, we despair, assuming God has signed off or that our receiving tower is defective.

Such nagging questions indicate that we are trapped in a Phase One Following paradigm. In describing the role of the Holy Spirit in our lives, Jesus wasn't suggesting we move into the spiritual CB age. He had something far more revolutionary in mind. Forget about being CB disciples. Jesus planned for us to become cellular disciples.

THE CALL TO CELLULAR DISCIPLESHIP

Although I've been using a cellular phone for some time now, I continue to be amazed by this breakthrough in technology, especially when I compare it to my previous experiences with CB communication. My cellular telephone offers dramatic improvements over my old CB radio.

▶ *Powerful Transmission.* My phone is tiny with a two-inch antenna, yet I can dial a number and talk with people across the country. In fact, if cost were no object, I could talk with people around the world.

▶ *No Party Lines.* When I want to talk with someone on my cellular phone, I don't have to battle inane chatter from others using the airwaves. At times, I may pick up some static, but it is nothing compared to the old CB "breaker 1-9" days.

▶ *Powerful and Simple Reception.* When someone wants to talk with me, it's easy. They dial. My phone rings. I answer. We talk. No matter where I am, when someone needs to reach me, I am accessible.

Both CB radios and cellular phones are communication tools. But if someone offered you a choice between the two with no difference in cost, which would you choose? Most people would say, "Bring on the cellular!" Why live with the limitations of old CB technology when something far better is available? It helps me to think of Phase Two Following as a continuum of spiritual communication ranging from CB discipleship to cellular discipleship. However, I don't want to push the analogy too far. No one has a direct-link cellular line to God that enables them to carry on static-free two-way conversations (no matter what some TV preachers claim). I do believe, however, that as spiritual followers, we can have a real relationship with God and communicate with Him. I believe there are steps we can take to enhance the quality of our communication with God so that it is less "CB-ish" and more cellular. How to progress on that continuum is our focus in part 4 of our study together.

An Offer They Could Not Refuse

Jesus offered His disciples a startling and powerful new way to follow Him. When He first described the Holy Spirit's work, the disciples missed the implications. Once the Holy Spirit came, however, they discovered that they could follow Jesus more effectively and more intimately than ever before. Yes, it was a different way of following, but it was a better way.

Even after Jesus returned to the Father and the disciples moved forward as Phase Two Followers, they must have had times when they longed to walk down a beach with Jesus and watch a sunrise. There's nothing wrong with that. At times, I wish for a Phase One relationship with Jesus with its "up close and personal" touch. In some ways, that experience stills sounds easier, possibly better. Yet I know Jesus said that what we have is the best option for now, so I'm learning to embrace the mystery of life as a Phase Two Follower.

In the remainder of part 4, we're going to explore life as Phase Two Followers. We're going to discover the role of written communication in this phase of following, the thrill and challenge of hearing God's voice, how to follow Jesus if you get disoriented temporarily, and what to do if you feel totally lost. Before we're through, I hope you'll embrace your privilege as a Phase Two Follower.

By the way, don't feel slighted because you didn't have the chance to be a Phase One Follower. God has something better for you. You see, Phase Two is not the final phase. There is one more to come: Phase Three Following, the best of all. All of us will have our opportunity for that "up close and personal" time with Jesus. The apostle Paul described it this way: "Now we see but a poor reflection as in a mirror; then we shall see face to face. Now I know in part; then I shall know fully, even as I am fully known" (1 Cor. 13:12).

One day we will see Jesus face to face. What we do now prepares us for what we will do then. Jesus' first disciples had it good, but we have it better. One day, we'll all experience the best. For now, our assignment is clear: become better Phase Two Followers. God has given us all we need to succeed, including an essential resource we'll examine next—a map. As we will discover, it's dangerous to follow a leader you cannot see if you don't have a map that serves as an objective guide to keep you on course. Fortunately, we have a totally reliable spiritual map available to us—if we will use it.

GOD'S POST-IT NOTES

*You can follow the leader by following
the leader's written directions.*

Three words change everything for my daughters: "Dad's in charge."
Our world wobbles on its axis. Gone is the stability and structure Lynn
Marie adds to our lives. Leaving the girls and me "home alone" has
always challenged my wife. For years, before leaving town, she tried
reminding me of the daily washing chores, the mail and trash requirements, the intricate carpool schedules, and the daily variations of all
aforementioned items. She talked, and I listened carefully. Yet when
she returned from her trip, she always seemed . . . well, disappointed. I
wrote it off as unrealistic expectations.

My approach to life is somewhat more relaxed than Lynn Marie's.
She tends to be more structured (spelled r-i-g-i-d). Occasionally, we
discuss how our marriage and parenting experiences have made biblical stories come alive for us. I explain the empathy I have developed
for the children of Israel living under the Old Testament law. She
shares her sympathy for Moses as he cared for a bunch of whiners who
refused to follow the rules.

After numerous well-intentioned but failed attempts to guide us
through being home alone, Lynn Marie finally recognized the truth: in
my heart, I was not deliberately ignoring her instructions. Actually, I
empathized with the apostle Paul in the New Testament when he said,
"I do not understand what I do. For what I want to do I do not do. . . .
For I have the desire to do what is good, but I cannot carry it out. For
what I do is not the good I want to do; no, the evil I do not want to
do—this is what I keep doing" (Rom. 7:15, 18–19).

That's when Lynn Marie devised the Kramp Family Post-It
Management System. She stopped rehearsing the regulations, requirements, and schedules with me before she left town. Instead, she wrote

it all down. On numerous Post-Its, she wrote all the things we were supposed to do while she was gone, organized them neatly for each day, and stuck them to the kitchen cabinet door by the telephone. To reinforce the plan, she placed reminder Post-Its in strategic locations: bathroom mirrors, bedroom doors, and the speedometer of my car.

The results were outstanding. In Lynn Marie's absence, the girls and I knew what we needed to do. Each day we removed Post-Its with great satisfaction, knowing we had met that day's requirements. The system has broken down at times, but overall the Post-It Management System has enabled our family unit to follow Lynn Marie's directions even when we are left home alone.

FOLLOWING THE WORDS OF JESUS

As Jesus prepared His disciples for Phase Two Following, He stressed the importance of His "word"—all that He said and taught. He expected the disciples to listen and apply His teaching to their lives. Jesus wanted them to understand that when they did what He said, they were following Him. Of course, this would be far more important when the disciples transitioned into Phase Two Following. Then the Holy Spirit would use the written Word to keep their lives on course. "'All this I have spoken while still with you. But the Counselor, the Holy Spirit, whom the Father will send in my name, will teach you all things and will remind you of everything I have said to you'" (John 14:25–26).

The Holy Spirit would become an internal Post-It system that would jog their memories at the precise moment they needed spiritual truth. To reinforce the importance of what He said, Jesus equated obedience with love—obeying His word demonstrated their love. On the other hand, affirming love for Him without doing what He said was a hopeless contradiction. "Jesus replied, 'If anyone loves me, he will obey my teaching. My Father will love him, and we will come to him and make our home with him. He who does not love me will not obey my teaching'" (John 14:23–24).

Jesus knew that His words would be written for future disciples to read, study, and apply in their lives. When His words were added to the complete revelation of the Bible, they would guide and govern His disciples' lives. Rather than a trite collection of religious writings, the

Old and New Testaments would become the perfect spiritual map by which disciples could navigate.

> For the word of God is living and active. Sharper than any double-edged sword, it penetrates even to dividing soul and spirit, joints and marrow; it judges the thoughts and attitudes of the heart. (Heb. 4:12)
>
> All Scripture is God-breathed and is useful for teaching, rebuking, correcting and training in righteousness, so that the man of God may be thoroughly equipped for every good work. (2 Tim. 3:16–17)

Under Phase Two Following, Jesus' disciples would have the spiritual map they needed to follow Him even though He would no longer be with them physically. In addition, His word would become the objective source of truth they could use to measure all other subjective spiritual communication (as we will see in the next chapter).

Following Jesus' Words Today

Despite unprecedented advances in communication technology and Christian publishing, there is a crisis today in biblical literacy. Many Christians have lost their spiritual maps or do not know how to use them. Inside and outside the church, people are uninformed, confused, or both. Not only do the finer points of theology puzzle them, but the central truths of the Christian faith jumble in their minds.

Although Jesus promised that the Holy Spirit would use His words to keep us on course, the Spirit does not dump biblical data into our minds like a download from a mainframe computer. It is our responsibility to read and understand the Bible. Only then can the Holy Spirit use those words to empower and transform us. If we want to develop our spiritual lives, here are some essential steps to take.

Know the story. We all need to know the basic biblical story beginning with the teachings of Jesus in the Gospels. From there we can expand our knowledge of the remainder of the New Testament and eventually the Old Testament. These inspired words become the basic data the Holy Spirit uses to help us follow Jesus.

Understand the story. It is important that we move beyond the basic facts and strive to understand what is said. At times, we become confused as we read the Bible, yet as we continue to study, the Holy Spirit will increase our understanding, and the mental fog will begin to lift.

Interpret the story correctly. Great damage is done when Christians misinterpret God's Word. God revealed His message within a context. To understand what the words mean, we must understand the context in which they were written. Fortunately, many excellent Bible study tools are available today to help us "rightly divide the word of truth." In addition, God has gifted many pastors, Bible teachers, and others to help us correctly interpret the more difficult passages.

Accept the complete story. The Bible is not a spiritual smorgasbord from which God invites us to pick and choose. All Scripture is inspired by God. That means the total biblical message becomes our spiritual map, and we must not set aside parts we find troublesome. Ignoring portions of a map doesn't change the realities it describes. It does, however, destroy our capability to navigate effectively. In the same way, to follow Jesus today, we need the complete map God has given us.

Jesus' words changed the lives of His first disciples as they will change our lives today. It is impossible, however, for us to follow Jesus apart from His written words. Yes, the Holy Spirit will guide and teach us, but we must read, understand, interpret, and apply the complete message to our lives.

THE NEED FOR OBJECTIVE DIRECTIONS

Although we operate as Phase Two Followers of Jesus, we can still determine objectively what Jesus is saying to us. In the same way that Jesus' disciples could hear Jesus speak, we can hear Him speak through the Bible. Everything else we believe God is saying to us must be measured against that objective revelation. Jesus would not say anything today through any sort of subjective means that contradicts what He has already said in the Bible. As a result, we have a "north star" to guide us.

Unfortunately, many Christians prefer their subjective communication with God to the objective revelation of the Bible. Rather than taking the time to learn what God has revealed in His Word, they focus on spiritual impressions, hunches, circumstances, open doors, opportunities, or whatever else they believe indicates that God is speaking to them. Other means of communication are fine, and God may use them at times to direct our lives. However, they must remain secondary to the biblical revelation.

The same problem can occur when Christians use the Bible. It's common these days for some people to say, "This morning as I was praying, God told me _____." Then to add credibility to their statement, they refer to a particular Scripture verse. Often it is clear they are misinterpreting the verse (probably unintentionally) to support their preconceived position. When I point out this problem, some say, "Well, this is what that verse means to me."

Frankly, it doesn't matter what a particular verse of Scripture means to any of us. God's Word means what it means. A particular passage of Scripture has only one meaning. Some passages are difficult to interpret, and even biblical scholars cannot agree on the one, correct interpretation. Scholarly disagreement does not mean, however, that a verse means multiple things. The lack of agreement simply indicates that we may not know the correct interpretation yet. This is far different from saying that a passage means one thing to Tom and something else to Sue and something entirely different to Bill. Such an approach leaves us with a spiritual map that can be constantly redrawn based on the whim of the person holding it while disregarding the objective reality.

The Bible, correctly interpreted, provides the objective foundation for our faith. As we seek to follow Jesus, we must start with God's written Word and then allow the Holy Spirit to use that truth to move our lives in the proper direction. The vast majority of the direction God gives us is recorded in the Bible, and we must take the time to use that spiritual map effectively.

Taking God's Word Seriously

We cannot become better followers of Jesus without making His Word a high priority in our lives. We should be thankful, however, that He has given us all the written revelation we need. As you will see, seeking on-the-spot revelation can be a bit unnerving. Let me explain by telling you a true story you may struggle to believe but nonetheless is true.

I was standing in the tiny guest bedroom in our house in Oregon admiring the coat of paint I had just applied. Suddenly, a series of words began to appear: six-inch-tall, handwritten blue letters, blurred but legible through the white paint, circling the top of the walls like a wallpaper border. I screamed for Lynn Marie to come, and we both stared in disbelief as the following cryptic message appeared:

JOHN * JOHN * JOHN * JOHN * JOHN * JOHN * JOHN

My wife looked at me and asked, "What have you done?" Initially, I thought she was asking what I had done to the paint. I could have answered that question. Then I realized she was not asking a home maintenance question; she was asking a theological question. Given the fact that my name had just appeared mysteriously around all four walls of our guest bedroom, her question was justified. As you know, such unusual communication is not without biblical precedent, and I immediately grasped the implications.

The Book of Daniel graphically records a similar incident of handwriting on a wall. King Belshazzar of Babylon gave a great banquet for a thousand of his nobles. To impress his guests, Belshazzar ordered servants to bring the gold and silver goblets his father had taken from the temple in Jerusalem so that his nobles, his wives, and his concubines might drink from them. The servants obeyed. As the guests drank, they praised their gods made out of gold, silver, bronze, iron, wood, and stone. Their revelry abruptly ended, however, when an unwelcome apparition suddenly appeared: "Suddenly the fingers of a human hand appeared and wrote on the plaster of the wall, near the lampstand in the royal palace. The king watched the hand as it wrote. His face turned pale and he was so frightened that his knees knocked together and his legs gave way" (Dan. 5:5–6).

The message that appeared on Belshazzar's wall was concise:

MENE, MENE, TEKEL, PARSIN

When the prophet Daniel translated the message for the king, it bode ill for Belshazzar's future. The heart of the message was this: "You have been weighed in the balance and found wanting." That night, a rival killed Belshazzar, and Darius took over his throne.

There in our guest bedroom, Belshazzar's unfortunate experience popped into my mind and Lynn Marie's question ("What did you do?")

hung unanswered. We consulted the highest authority we knew: a local painter named Ray. He walked into the bedroom and stared at the wall. I described my painting process and the mysterious way my name had appeared and circled the room. After a few minutes he asked, "So your name just appeared on the wall?" "Yes," I replied earnestly. "All I did was paint." Ray stared at the wall for a moment then said, "When this happens, it's generally not good news."

Initially, I thought Ray was offering his professional assessment as a painter. Yet when he and Lynn Marie began laughing, I realized that Ray had joined her in rendering his theological assessment. Leave it to me to get a painter who knew the story of Belshazzar!

Ray and Lynn Marie were not the last ones to enjoy a good laugh at my expense as word spread about the mysterious, on-the-spot revelation on my wall. Later, I discovered that my problem was not sin but paint. The teenage daughter of the previous owners of our house had a boyfriend named John. She wrote his name in blue markers like a border around her room. Before selling the home, the family discovered that the water soluble marker seeped through light colored paint so they painted the room the color of the marker. My fresh coat of white paint brought the marker ink to the surface once again.

Before that experience, I had wished occasionally that God would reveal His will to me in a unique way, perhaps by writing it on the wall. Never again. My experience in my guest bedroom cured me. The Bible is all the written revelation I need.

20 THE SPIRITUAL HEARING AID

You can follow the leader by listening to the leader's voice.

My Grandpa Frachiseur raised cattle in Arkansas. When asked about his work he would say, "I've messed with cows my whole life. Why if you cut me, I'd probably bleed cow blood." As a child, I believed him and was convinced he had some sort of magical power over cattle.

I developed this theory while riding with Grandpa in his dirty green, creaky pickup truck through the pasture to feed the cows. After easing over the cattle-guard, we bounced along the rutted road leading to the barn. Most times the pastures were empty—not a bull, cow, or calf in sight. Then Grandpa would lean out the window and bellow a unique sound, a series of tones which began with the surprised "Caaaaah" of a large crow landing on a thorn bush; then shifted to the sustained "AAAAA" of a camper taking an icy shower; and ended abruptly with a rising "eeaaaAAH" of an opera singer swallowing a fly at the peak of the climatic high note. If you would like to try this in the privacy of your own home, here's an audio map for your use: CaaaaahAAAAAeeeaaaAAH.

As soon as Grandpa sounded the call, cattle appeared from every direction, trotting out of the woods and up from the river bottoms. They formed lines behind the pickup as we continued our bouncy ride toward the barn. When we stopped, the herd of cattle faced us like a mob at the cafeteria following a Sunday morning church service.

As I grew older, I discovered that Grandpa's distinctive call, rather than magic, lured those cattle. They associated that sound with the one who fed and cared for them. They recognized Grandpa's voice and looked for him every time they heard it.

In Jesus' day, people knew about sheep and shepherds instead of cattle, so He used that knowledge to help them understand spiritual truths about hearing God's voice. First, He described His relationship to them as a shepherd: "I am the good shepherd. The good shepherd lays down his life for the sheep. The hired hand is not the shepherd who owns the sheep. So when he sees the wolf coming, he abandons the sheep and runs away. Then the wolf attacks the flock and scatters it" (John 10:11–12).

Jesus used the same analogy to illustrate that His followers would be able to recognize His voice the way sheep can recognize the voice of their shepherd: "The man who enters by the gate is the shepherd of his sheep. The watchman opens the gate for him, and the sheep listen to his voice. He calls his own sheep by name and leads them out. When he has brought out all his own, he goes on ahead of them, and his sheep follow him because they know his voice. But they will never follow a stranger; in fact, they will run away from him because they do not recognize a stranger's voice" (John 10:2–5).

The application of Jesus' parable was clear: His disciples needed a relationship with Him that ensured they would recognize His voice and follow when He called. Years earlier when King David tried to describe his relationship with God, he also used the language of a sheep and shepherd.

> The Lord is my shepherd, I shall not be in want. He makes me lie down in green pastures, he leads me beside quiet waters, he restores my soul. He guides me in paths of righteousness for his name's sake. Even though I walk through the valley of the shadow of death, I will fear no evil, for you are with me; your rod and your staff, they comfort me. You prepare a table before me in the presence of my enemies. You anoint my head with oil; my cup overflows. Surely goodness and love will follow me all the days of my life, and I will dwell in the house of the LORD forever. (Ps. 23)

As our Good Shepherd, Jesus leads us, cares for us, and protects us. We have a relationship with Him that involves ongoing communication. Undoubtedly, Jesus' disciples understood how this relationship functioned while they were with Him physically, yet struggled to grasp how it would work in the future. Fortunately for them (and for us), Jesus was prepared to help them make the adjustment.

New Skills for a New Phase of Following

The challenge for Jesus was weaning His disciples from Phase One Following and preparing them for Phase Two Following. They and all future followers would need to discern His voice as He spoke to them in new ways once the Holy Spirit came. Yet these new means of communication would create special challenges.

For example, when Jesus spoke during His earthly ministry, people could see and hear Him. They may have disagreed about the interpretation of His message, but no one argued over the fact that He had spoken. This would not be true in Phase Two Following, as Jesus' communication moved from an objective to a subjective reality. Rather than simply disputing the content of His message, future followers could disagree on whether they believed Jesus had actually spoken. For the first time, one follower could say, "The Lord said this to me," and another follower could say, "I don't believe Jesus would say something like that." Fortunately, God understands this struggle and has been working to help people tune in to His voice throughout history.

Recognizing the Voice of God

We do not automatically discern God's voice, but we can learn to do so because God takes the initiative to help us. That's the good news we discover in the story of the young boy Samuel in the Old Testament.

Samuel lived in a place of worship with an old spiritual leader named Eli. One night, after the two of them lay down to sleep, the Lord spoke to Samuel. Thinking that Eli had called him, Samuel ran to Eli's room and said, "Here I am; you called me?" But Eli said, "I didn't call you; go back and lie down." It happened a second time. Samuel went to Eli, and Eli sent him back to bed. When it happened the third time, Eli realized something important was happening in the life of his young apprentice, so he gave Samuel some specific instructions: "Then Eli realized that the Lord was calling the boy. So Eli told Samuel, "Go and lie down, and if he calls you, say, "Speak, Lord, for your servant is listening."" So Samuel went and lay down in his place. The Lord came and stood there, calling as at the other times, 'Samuel! Samuel!' Then Samuel said, 'Speak, for your servant is listening'" (1 Sam. 3:8–10).

Eli realized that Samuel was beginning the incredible adventure of hearing and responding to the voice of God. From the biblical record, we discover that Samuel learned his lesson well. He served the nation throughout his life as a wise spiritual leader who clearly discerned God's plan and directions.

Most of us believe what the Bible says about Samuel's experience and understand Jesus' analogy of the sheep and the shepherd, but we still have a basic question: How can average, ordinary people today know when God is speaking to them?

Although our primary spiritual map is the objective revelation of the Bible, discipleship is more than a left-brain, analytical exercise focused entirely on Bible study. There is also a right-brain dimension to following Jesus that is creative and intuitive. Here are some important subjective means God uses to speak to us and direct our lives today.

Our feelings and emotions. God created us as emotional beings so we can experience His presence in our lives on an emotional level. The Holy Spirit uses emotions such as "a sense of peace," or "a sense of uneasiness" as directional signs that help us follow Jesus. As a result, how we feel about certain situations can become one of the ways God communicates with us.

Our desires and aspirations. God sometimes directs us by placing the desire in us to do certain things that please and honor Him. When that desire is energized by the Holy Spirit, the motivation that results can become a tool God uses to communicate with us and help us follow Him.

Our opportunities and roadblocks. When opportunities come for us to do certain things or to pursue a certain course, God may be directing us. In the same way, when we encounter roadblocks, God may be redirecting and protecting us. The combination of opportunities and roadblocks can help us discern God's direction for our lives during important times of decision.

Our capabilities and successes. As we understand the spiritual gifts God has given us and reflect on how He has accomplished His work through us by using those gifts, we can often discern God's plans for us in the future. God always prepares us for the places to which He leads us and gifts us for what He calls us to do.

Our interaction with other believers. God accomplishes His work through His body on earth, the church. He wants us to experience true fellowship with other Christians so that we can learn from them and join them to accomplish tasks we could not do alone. Often, we can hear God's voice through the insights He gives other Christians. God values diversity. Although we may struggle to understand and even appreciate the viewpoints of other Christians, we cannot afford to isolate ourselves from them, for in doing so we may lose a perspective we need to understand what God is doing around us.

Our weaknesses and failures. Sometimes, we can hear God's voice more clearly when we fail than when we succeed—although we may not like what we're hearing! During times when we struggle, feel drained, or lack joy in what we do, we may experience God's gracious leadership. Many times God leads us into difficult situations so that He can get our attention and guide us in new directions. We must learn to embrace situations that highlight our weaknesses and leave us with a sense of failure since these may be means God uses to communicate truths to us we cannot hear any other way.

Because these means of spiritual communication are subjective, we can easily misunderstand them. As a result, we should never rely on them as the primary way we receive direction from God. The writer of Proverbs offered good advice in this area: "Trust in the LORD with all your heart and lean not on your own understanding; in all your ways acknowledge him, and he will make your paths straight" (Prov. 3:5–6). This verse reminds us of the balance we need with both objective and subjective communication with God.

Objective Communication. Because of God's revelation to us in the Bible, we have a spiritual map we can use as we seek to follow Him. By building a solid foundation of biblical truth in our lives, we can evaluate anything else we believe God is saying to us. The Bible provides the over-arching direction for our lives. Many times, Scripture cannot tell us the specific decision we need to make when several options are within the scope of God's Word. But the Bible can help us know immediately if we are out of bounds. God never contradicts Himself, so His written Word will never conflict with something He says in another way.

Subjective Communication. God often uses other means to help us discern the specific actions we need to take and the decisions we need to make. We can examine our emotions, our abilities and gifts, our opportunities, and even our failures to discover how (or if) God is using them to direct us. Once we validate this subjective communication with the objective revelation of the Bible, we can be confident that we have heard God's voice and can respond in obedience.

The good news we learn from the Old Testament story of Samuel as well as Jesus' illustration about the good shepherd is that God takes the initiative to communicate with us. He understands our limitations and finds a way to get His message to us. Yes, as followers, we are responsible for hearing His voice, but our responsibility is based on His initiative. God communicates; then we listen and respond.

Turning Up Our Spiritual Hearing Aids

As Phase Two Followers of Jesus Christ, we face the profound challenge of following a leader we cannot see. To do so, we must make hearing Jesus' voice one of the highest priorities in our lives. That means that we cannot afford to respond the way my grandmother did when she got tired of listening to someone.

Grandmother Kramp was hard of hearing and wore a large hearing aid with a volume control. My grandfather always complained that she didn't fight fair. When they argued, Grandmother would deliver her verbal punches and then turn off her hearing aid, ending further discussion. Grandmother refused to hear anything she didn't want to hear. When she was through listening, she tuned out.

In our relationship with Jesus, we need to hear from Him whenever and however He chooses to communicate with us. We must listen to what He says even if He tells us things we would rather not hear. As spiritual people living in a physical world, we are all "hard of hearing." Fortunately, God has equipped us, through His Spirit, to hear His voice.

In the Book of Revelation, Jesus spoke to the early Christians and challenged them to remain sensitive to His voice and keep the door of fellowship open: "Here I am! I stand at the door and knock. If anyone hears my voice and opens the door, I will come in and eat with him, and he with me" (Rev. 3:20).

Our communication with Jesus is part of an authentic relationship. We can know Him, love Him, and hear Him. At times, we may allow barriers to develop in our relationship with Him, but even then Jesus stands at the door and knocks . . . and knocks . . . and knocks. As

God did with Samuel in Old Testament times, Jesus takes the initiative to communicate with us today. So keep that spiritual hearing aid on with the volume cranked high. Then when Jesus speaks, be prepared to listen and follow.

LEARNING THE WAY BY KNOWING THE LEADER

The better you know the leader,
the easier it is to follow.

The light turned red as the van ahead of us zipped through the intersection, turned left, and quickly vanished in the rain and traffic. It was 6:05 A.M.

"Will Granddaddy wait for us?" asked Kelly, my younger daughter from the back seat of our van. Even though she was only seven years old at the time, she understood that it was going to be tough for us to follow my father if we were stuck at the traffic light.

The plan had been simple and foolproof. My father, Bill, in Van #1 (joined by my mother and sister) was going to lead the way to Santa Fe, New Mexico. My family in Van #2 was going to follow. We had backed out of my parents' driveway at 6:04 A.M. Even that represented a minor victory for my father, who would have preferred for us to sleep in the vans to ensure a punctual departure at 6:00 A.M. as planned. In spite of rebellious travelers and a furious thunderstorm that rumbled through Dallas that morning, Big Bill got the trip underway almost on schedule. Like so many road trips before it, another Kramp family trek was off to a grand start with Big Bill in the lead. Then I got stuck at that red light.

After minutes that stretched without mercy, the light turned green. Quickly, I raced down Centerville Road where we connected with I-635 and then onto I-30 through downtown Dallas. Although my father and I had not discussed specific travel plans (since I planned to follow him), I knew he had to go through Ft. Worth. So if I could catch him, we could resume our original plan: he could lead; I would follow.

Although the particular "following" situation that confronted me that morning was new, I had a lifetime of experience following my father. Based on what I had seen him do in the past, I had to anticipate what he would do in this specific situation.

My first thought was that he would recognize that we were not behind him, pull over to the side of the road, and wait for us. For several minutes, I stared through rain and headlights searching for the red, flashing tail-lights of his van. In time I ruled out that option. Due to heavy traffic, I reasoned, it would be dangerous to pull over; therefore, I believed Big Bill would keep driving.

Then I became concerned that my father had circled back to find us. If so, I could be in front of the leader and would never find him. I ruled out that option as stupid, something a roadmaster like my father would never do. Instinctively, I sensed Van #1 was still somewhere ahead of us. If that were the case, I knew my father would be trying to contact me on the CB radio. As I drove, I grasped the CB microphone and repeated "break for Big Bill; break for Big Bill." Every lightning flash filled the radio with static, but I didn't give up. I knew my father would be listening.

As the morning rush-hour traffic snared and held me captive, I kept thinking, "What will my father do?" Without being able to explain why, I just knew that he would continue driving slowly while using his radio to contact me. He would expect me to keep moving toward Ft. Worth and to catch up with him.

How did I "know" this? Well, I didn't actually "know" it. For years I had been with my father in a variety of situations. I knew the way he thought and responded. Now in this new situation I was guessing what he would do based on all I knew about him. Without realizing it at the time, I was drawing on a fundamental followism: The better you know the leader, the easier it is to follow the leader. A close relationship with the leader is important in any following situation but essential if you attempt to follow a leader you cannot see.

ANTICIPATING JESUS' ACTIVITY

As followologists, we can anticipate Jesus' activity today by studying what He did and said in the first century as recorded in the Bible. As Phase Two Followers, we can use our knowledge of Jesus' activities and priorities two thousand years ago to determine general principles that will help us follow Him now.

Throughout His ministry, Jesus stayed on the move. He was not frantic; instead He moved with purpose. In fact, constant activity was an essential part of His plan for training His disciples. Like a great film director, Jesus changed scenes constantly, searching for the ideal setting for the teaching or ministry experience His disciples needed.

Rather than waiting for the spectacular moment or the "big event," Jesus utilized the ordinary circumstances of life. When invited, He went to weddings and parties. On the Sabbath, He went to the synagogue. For the holiday festivals, He went to Jerusalem. When possible, He spent time in the region in which He had been raised. At times Jesus sought solitude, especially when He wanted private time with His disciples and personal time to pray. Yet He welcomed people into His life and ministered to their needs. When we survey His life with a broad view, we can identify these overarching principles that seemed to guide what He did:

- ▶ He valued motion and activity and viewed purposeful action as an essential part of His master training plan for His followers.

- ▶ He celebrated the common events of life and used them as the primary backdrop for His ministry rather than waiting for the spectacular moments.

- ▶ He sought solitude and made time for prayer and personal renewal.

- ▶ He welcomed people into His life and ministered to them, especially those who were hurting and had no one else to help them.

These overarching principles become landmarks that help us orient ourselves as Phase Two Followers of Jesus today. Since Jesus is the same yesterday, today, and forever, we can anticipate that He will do today what He did then.

Watching for Jesus at Work Today

If you lost sight of Jesus today, where would you look for Him? We must draw on all we know about Jesus to help us recognize His activity around us today. Here is an expanded set of signposts we can use:

Expect action. We should expect Jesus to be at work constantly around us. The pace and scope of His ministry on earth was incredible during Phase One. But now as the Holy Spirit works through the lives of Christians—Jesus' body on earth—there is no limit to what He can do and where He can work.

Expect variety. We should expect Him to work in many different ways. As we consider His global presence, we must open our minds to the awesome breadth of His activity. Jesus is working with people in settings we would never anticipate and in ways that may startle us. Rather than resisting the new and unfamiliar, we must be watchful and ready to join Jesus wherever He is working and in whatever way He is accomplishing His work.

Monitor the common situations. On earth, Jesus did some of His best work in the midst of normal activities. As we seek to follow Him today, we should look for His activity where we work, in our homes, and in our neighborhoods. Certainly, Jesus often works in organized settings and even in staged extravaganzas, but we must never forget His preference for working wonders in the ordinary moments of life.

Watch for people with needs. If Jesus' disciples got separated from Him, they could usually find Him with people—especially with people who were hurting. We need to embrace that truth. Rather than viewing needy people as problems to be avoided, we should view them as signposts to Jesus. If we lose sight of Jesus, we should look for the hurting people around us. There is a good chance those people will lead us straight to Him.

Check the quiet places. When Jesus was not with people, He was alone with His Heavenly Father in prayer. As we seek Him today, we should not overlook the quiet places of solitude. In our hustle-bustle world, we must take time to join Him away from the noise and the crowds.

Big Signs We Cannot Miss

If you have ever traveled on Interstate Highway 10 through Arizona, you've seen the signs for "The Thing." In the middle of nowhere, signs appear that say something like, "Only 608 miles to 'The Thing.'" Initially, it's easy to ignore the signs. Who cares about seeing "The Thing" anyway—whatever it is. But the signs don't stop. Before long there's another sign: "Only 583 miles to 'The Thing.'" More miles; more signs. "Only 443 miles to 'The Thing.'" As you draw closer, the signs become more frequent, counting the miles in smaller and smaller increments. Ultimately, there are signs that indicate how many more yards until you get to "The Thing." Finally, just before the exit, there is one last sign that says, "Exit here for 'The Thing.'" Just past that exit is a sign that says, "Go back. You just missed 'The Thing.'" After reading those signs for several hours and hundreds of miles, it takes a strong-willed driver to pass that exit. I succumbed. I stopped. I paid my quarter and saw "The Thing." It was worth a quarter—not much more, but definitely worth a quarter for the entertainment value of the signs alone. One thing was for sure: everyone driving down that highway knew about "The Thing." There was no way to miss it.

Fortunately, Jesus leaves signs today for us to follow—big letters with bold type that we cannot miss. It's good to know that if the general principles we have already identified are not enough to help us spot Jesus at work around us, there are some surefire signs that point us in the right direction every time.

A non-Christian asking questions about God. This is one of the clearest signs that the Spirit is moving in a person's life. People do not seek God on their own initiative, so if they start asking spiritual questions, pay attention. Immediately drop what you're doing and give them directions. God is at work there and you can be part of what He is doing.

A Christian seeking a deeper relationship with God. In the Christian life, it's easy to become complacent. So when Christians seek ways to move deeper in their relationships with God, it's clear that God is at work. Help them if you can. Better yet, join them and develop your relationship with God together. Once again, you'll find yourself in the middle of something Jesus is doing right now.

People meeting needs in the name of Christ. Selfishness runs deep in our lives. In contrast, God has special concern for the widow, the orphan, the prisoner, the hungry, the blind, and others in need. So when you see people setting aside their personal needs to meet the needs of others, support them. They are doing work that flows from the heart of God. Join them, and you will move into the center of God's activity.

Christians striving for unity with spiritual integrity. Jesus told us the Father values unity among His children. When Christians work to bring believers together without trivializing the truths that cannot be compromised, pay attention. Encourage them; pray for them. The Father is pleased when His children play together nicely. Don't miss out and, by all means, don't spoil it! Get involved with them and you can be confident that you are moving closer to Jesus.

Christians orienting their lives around God's values. When you see people living in ways that reflect God's value system, take notice. Watch for people moving to the end of the line rather than the front. Serving rather than sitting. Giving rather than hoarding. Building up rather than tearing down. Turning a cheek rather than striking back. Seeking the lost rather than counting the saved. People do not develop Kingdom values unless the King works in their hearts. When you see them, run to join them. Without a doubt, they are emissaries of the King and you want to be part of His entourage.

Are there other evidences of God's work? Sure. Plenty. The ones I've listed are the no-brainers, the ones we can't miss. The better we know Jesus, the more we can anticipate what He will do in our world today.

STILL CHASING VAN #1

Remember my problem of being separated from my father in Dallas? As I told you, I had settled on a basic plan: keep driving and stay tuned to the radio. After more than forty-five minutes of frustration, I heard a faint but wonderful CB sound: "Break for John. Break for John. Come back."

Minutes later, our two vans reconnected. No space shuttle commander has ever been more pleased to "dock" his vehicle in orbit than I was to pull behind Van #1 that morning. At the next exit, both vans pulled off for an emergency stop so all parties could address physical needs brought on by more than an hour of leading-and-following stress. We were soon on the road again with Big Bill in the lead and me following close behind. After a tense morning, I was thankful I knew my father well enough to anticipate his actions so I could find and follow him again. Without that experience to guide me, I might still be circling Dallas!

Let's do the same thing with Jesus as our spiritual leader. Deepening our relationship with Jesus determines our ability to follow Him. Let's go deeper so we can follow better!

22

FOLLOWING
IN THE DARK

*When it's dark, stand still
and trust the leader.*

Amateur spelunkers never forget Carlsbad Caverns in New Mexico. Since the Park Service opened the caves to the public in 1923, thousands of people have walked through the majestic underground world of mountains, "bottomless" pits, water pools, stalactites, and stalagmites. For decades, families have gathered at sunset to watch swarms of bats spew from the cave like a twisting cloud of smoke into the desert sky.

One year, my parents included Carlsbad in our family vacation. As the oldest of three children, I wanted to be brave, but as an eight-year-old, the winding walk down the throat of Carlsbad gave me the creeps. As the cave swallowed us, I consoled myself by watching the park rangers who guided us into the foreboding underworld. The rangers, decked in chocolate brown uniforms and carrying powerful flashlights, surely knew the way. Squeezing through the crowd, I moved beside the first ranger and stuck to his side like fuzz on Velcro.

The head ranger entertained us during our winding descent by telling us all sorts of helpful information about cave life. For example, he explained how to remember the difference between stalactites (they must hold *tight* to the ceiling) and stalagmites (they *might* reach the ceiling if they grow taller). Using his powerful flashlight to focus our attention on the deepest recesses of the cave where millions of bats lived, the ranger described the cave floor covered with five to ten feet of bat guano (technically called bat excrement). He explained the challenge newborn bats face as they learn to fly. After spending their early days clinging in clumps by the thousands to the ceiling, the baby bats turn loose (or get pushed) and have one chance to fly.

146

The successful ones flit; the unsuccessful ones splat into a giant mound of guano. Even as a child, I imagined that would be a tough way to go.

Finally, the ranger taught us about the power of darkness. As we sat on benches, he explained that all cave creatures are blind. The absence of light blinds every living thing (including people) that remains in the cave for an extended period of time. Then after warning us to remain seated, he switched off the lights so we could experience the total darkness of Carlsbad. In the moments that followed, my child's mind generated an explosion of questions. What if the lights didn't come back on? What if we became blind? Worse yet, what if the rangers became blind? Then who would lead us?

Everyone remained absolutely still—children and adults. Intellectually, we knew the ranger was still there, yet emotion overpowered logic. We did the only thing we could do—nothing. In silence, we trusted the leader to take care of us in the darkness, to do for us what we could not do for ourselves. Emotional distress ended quickly as the ranger turned on the lights and continued our tour.

Recently, a friend told me that when he took the cave tour soon after Carlsbad opened to the public, the rangers turned off the lights and played a tape of the old hymn "Rock of Ages, Cleft for Me." Apparently, the combination of total darkness and somber music provided a more intense experience than most tourists wanted, so the park service discontinued the music. I agree with those early spelunkers. Who needs music? For me, those moments of total darkness were unforgettable.

Discipleship Darkness

As a child I experienced the power of physical darkness in Carlsbad. Years later, I would discover darkness in the spiritual realm that frightened and disoriented me far more. Not the darkness of evil but the absence of light when we cannot sense God's presence. One writer described it this way: "In his book for pastors, *The Living Reminder*, Henri Nouwen coins a remarkable and daring phrase: 'the ministry of absence.' Ministers do a disservice, he says, if they witness only to God's presence and do not prepare others to experience the times when God seems absent."[8]

As we have seen, Jesus provided His disciples all they needed to follow Him after He ascended into heaven. The Holy Spirit would live in their hearts, helping them discern spiritual truth and energizing them to act on that truth. His word, ultimately in written form, would become their spiritual map. Through a variety of other means, He would give them spiritual guidance to make decisions when biblical passages did not address their specific concerns. With these collective resources, Jesus' disciples would be equipped to follow Him even when they could not see Him physically. Yet Jesus knew there would be times when circumstances would overwhelm them and these spiritual resources would seem inadequate. There would be times when His followers would feel isolated, deserted, and immobilized by spiritual darkness. Somehow, Jesus had to prepare them for those Phase Two Following challenges.

The Big Plunge with the Lights Out

To prepare them for the crisis of darkness, Jesus led His disciples into situations that overwhelmed and disoriented them: storms at sea that threatened their lives, hungry crowds that demanded food, and a friend who slipped into death and back to life again. In each of these situations and others, Jesus demonstrated that He could handle anything they faced in life or in death. Over time, their faith grew and their willingness to face difficult circumstances increased. But nothing could prepare them fully for what was going to happen. When the days of darkness came, every disciple faltered. But for one of them, the spiritual darkness of the crucifixion dealt a crushing blow.

Thomas was prepared to follow Jesus through the fire. He was not prepared, however, to follow Jesus through the darkness. Even as Jesus walked toward Jerusalem to face the final crisis in His ministry, Thomas stated that he would gladly pay the ultimate price of discipleship. We have no reason to think he was insincere. It is clear, though, that Thomas anticipated pain but not doubt. As a result, when Jesus died on the cross, faith died for Thomas. He would have fought enemy soldiers, but he surrendered to the enemies of doubt that besieged his heart.

Three days later when the other disciples reported that they had seen Jesus resurrected from the dead, Thomas refused to believe it. The loss had been too great; the disappointment too intense. The darkness overwhelmed his resolve to risk faith once again. "So the other disciples told him, 'We have seen the Lord!' But he said to them, 'Unless I see the nail marks in his hands and put my finger where the nails were, and put my hand into his side, I will not believe it'" (John 20:25).

Jesus recognized the depth of Thomas's pain and treated his wounds with the ointment of grace. Jesus suddenly appeared as the disciples met behind locked doors and spoke directly to Thomas: "Then he said to Thomas, 'Put your finger here; see my hands. Reach out your hand and put it into my side. Stop doubting and believe.'" (John 20:27)

Thomas did believe, and Jesus was pleased. Yet even as He affirmed Thomas, Jesus stated the basis on which future followers would be blessed: "Then Jesus told him, 'Because you have seen me, you have believed; blessed are those who have not seen and yet have believed'" (John 20:29).

The future of Christianity, Jesus declared, depended on whether His disciples could believe and trust in what they couldn't see. Faith—a quiet confidence in God's presence and power—would be the essential capability that would enable them to survive the periods of darkness.

Facing Darkness in Phase Two Following

Although the darkness of the cross overwhelmed them, the disciples ultimately faced the darkness of suffering and opposition without faltering. For example, after Jesus' ascension into heaven, the Jewish religious leaders called the apostles before the council and ordered them not to preach in the name of Jesus again. The apostles flatly refused, so the religious leaders ordered that they be flogged. Strapped to a post with whips slicing their backs, it would have been easy to feel deserted by God in the darkness once again. But look how they responded this time: "The apostles left the Sanhedrin, rejoicing because they had been counted worthy of suffering disgrace for the Name. Day after day, in the temple courts and from house to house, they never stopped teaching and proclaiming the good news that Jesus is the Christ" (Acts 5:41–42).

The apostles actually rejoiced that they had the privilege of suffering for Jesus. Although they could not understand fully what God was doing through that situation, they trusted Him to accomplish something good. Armed with this quiet confidence, they faced whatever God allowed to come their way, whether seasons of light or darkness.

TESTIMONY FROM THE DARKNESS

For almost five years, my wife and I worked to begin a new church in a suburb of Portland, Oregon. In many ways, we loved those years. God gave us wonderful friends, insights into secular people, and a context in which our marriage and family grew even stronger. At the same time, those were the hardest years we have faced as a couple and certainly the toughest period of my life in ministry. I recognize that comparatively speaking we endured minor league hardships. The struggles faced by Christians and missionaries around the world make our situation pale in comparison. Yet any period of discipleship darkness is intensely significant for the one engulfed in it.

Those years brought me to a spiritual crisis. In my heart, one central question recurred: "God, where are You?" I had moved my family across the country to do what I thought God had "called" me to do. I could not understand why we were not more effective or why we struggled as we did.

That was when I read Philip Yancey's book *Disappointment with God*.[9] The title and content of his book gave me words to describe what I was feeling. My faith was intact. I was not angry with God. My emotion lodged deeper than anger. Yancey had it right; I was disappointed in God. I felt abandoned, frightened, and confused.

Darkness breeds questions like stagnant pools breed mosquitoes. Had I done something wrong, I wondered, to cause the problems we faced? Was there something new I needed to try? Why couldn't I *hear* God more clearly? Why couldn't I see God at work around me? Why was He allowing me and my family to endure this experience?

As I had done as a child in the darkness of Carlsbad Caverns, I strained harder to see a hint of spiritual light. But the wider I opened my eyes the more darkness I saw. Like the first disciples, I simply stood in the darkness. So when an opportunity came for me to begin a new ministry in Christian publishing, my wife and I accepted it as God's outstretched hand to us. A new challenge, yes, but also a way out of the darkness. At least that is what we hoped.

My darkness, unfortunately, remained encased in my life, and I took it across the country with me. My dream had been to begin a new church in Portland that would have an effective witness for years to come. But in spite of the fact that we and many others had worked hard and done all we knew to do, the church floundered. In light of the resources invested in that dream, my sense of failure was numbing. Wounded and discouraged, I had no idea what God was doing with my life or how He was leading me. All I could do was trust Him.

To my amazement, encouraging things began to happen. Five months into my new job, I was swept up in a massive reorganization in my new company and given greater opportunities and responsibilities than I could have imagined. In that new position, I could use gifts and abilities that were neither used nor valued in my work as a pastor.

Shortly thereafter, God led me to Mike Hyatt, a literary agent in Nashville. Over the next months, we became friends and I told him about my interest in writing. He read some of my material and listened to my unusual ideas about Lostology. Because of his encouragement and guidance, less than two years after I left Oregon, my first book, *Out of Their Faces and Into Their Shoes*, was published. To my surprise, it was a finalist for the Gold Medallion Award given by the Evangelical Christian Publishers Association.

For our family, our years in Nashville have been wonderful. Our girls have thrived in school and in the church we attend. Lynn Marie has become involved in her "first love" ministry: working with international students. God has overwhelmed us and carried us in a stream of grace.

Even now, with several years behind me to add perspective, I'm still struggling to understand all that God tried to teach me about following Him through the darkness. Plus I cannot understand why He led me out of the darkness into a period of great joy while other faithful Christians continue to struggle. While answers elude me, one thing has changed: my confidence in God is greater than ever before. I now understand that periods of darkness are part of Phase Two Following. And when those inevitable times come, God is with us in the darkness. Sometimes He leads us out of the darkness into a brighter time. Other times, He may accomplish His purposes by leaving us in the darkness. I do know this: We are never alone. So when it gets dark, we can stand still, reach for His hand, and trust Him. He is there. No matter how we feel or what we see.

STANDING WITH OTHERS IN THE DARKNESS

One of the greatest disciples of all time, John the Baptist, faced a period of darkness that makes my experience inconsequential. From his prison cell, John sent his disciples to Jesus with a simple question, a desperate cry of one man staring into the darkness and seeing nothing: "When John heard in prison what Christ was doing, he sent his disciples to ask him, 'Are you the one who was to come, or should we expect someone else?' Jesus replied, 'Go back and report to John what you hear and see: The blind receive sight, the lame walk, those who have leprosy are cured, the deaf hear, the dead are raised, and the good news is preached to the poor. Blessed is the man who does not fall away on account of me'" (Matt. 11:2–6).

Jesus didn't rebuke John for what he couldn't see. He realized that the darkness of circumstances had blurred John's spiritual vision. Rather than challenging John to try harder and to see more, Jesus became John's eyes. What a report Jesus sent to John. Blind people with 20-20 vision. Lame people running laps. Lepers with baby-soft skin. Deaf people eavesdropping on whispered conversations. People who had been dead now joining their families for dinner.

The report did not change John's circumstances. The outer darkness continued as Herod toyed with him, and death waited in the wings at the tyrant's whim. We don't know if the spiritual darkness lifted fully for John, but I believe Jesus' report rekindled his faith. With that faith he faced the unseen, forced his way through the darkness, and broke through to God's light. He was not the first nor the last to do so. Philip Yancey testifies of his battle through such a period in the darkness:

> Still, again and again I find the old amnesia creeping back, often accompanied by a haunting sense of God's absence. For one whole year, my prayers seemed to go nowhere; I never had the sense that God was listening. No minister had prepared me for the ordeal. In desperation I bought a "Book of Hours" used in high-church liturgy, and for that year I simply read the prayers and Bible passages, offering them to God as my prayers since I had no words of my own. I now look back on that time of absence as an

important period, for in some ways, I pursued God more earnestly than ever.[10]

In the darkness, God is not absent. He is actually closer to us than ever. The darkness impairs our perception of His presence, but if that leads us to pursue God more desperately, holding out hands of faith to touch His unseen hand, then the darkness can prompt spiritual growth. God is there. All the time. Nothing, even the darkness, can change that.

YOUR LIFE AS A FOLLOWOLOGIST

Followism 23:   *You can help others follow as you follow the leader.*

Followism 24:   *Following Jesus makes life meaningful.*

Don't Look Now, but You're Being Followed

23

*You can help others follow
as you follow the leader.*

Most people do not think of themselves as leaders. Yet as follow-ologists, we accept the fact that some people will follow us. In most cases, our role of leadership will be informal rather than structured. Either way, our assignment is straightforward and can be summarized in this statement: *Follow me, as I follow Christ.* Notice how this principle separates what we do as disciples from what others do in all other types of leadership.

> ▶ Our first responsibility as Christians is to follow Christ. If we are not doing that, we have nothing of value to offer other people.

> ▶ If we are following Christ, other people can learn more about following Jesus as they follow us.

> ▶ We need to help people focus on following Jesus. He must become their ultimate leader. Our goal is to get out of the way so they can have a clear view of Jesus.

> ▶ We cannot lead others to follow Jesus further than we have followed Him ourselves. Simply stated, we can't lead people where we have not been with Jesus.

> ▶ If we stop following Jesus for whatever reason, we must discourage others from following us. Obviously, it is dangerous to lead others when we do not know the way.

The apostle Paul first articulated this succinct leadership principle. The Christians in Corinth had become confused about who to follow and why. As he addressed their concerns, Paul defined the essential criteria for spiritual leadership. Using his own life as an example, he expressed the principle that would guide leaders and followers in the future: "Follow my example, as I follow the example of Christ" (1 Cor. 11:1).

Paul had committed his life to following Jesus—anywhere, any time, all the time. He demonstrated that commitment tirelessly and sacrificially; as a result, he challenged others to follow him as a Christian leader. Nonetheless, his explicit statement contained an implicit warning: Follow me only if I am following Jesus. Paul recognized that apart from his relationship with Jesus there was no reason for others to follow him.

Much of Paul's strength as a leader came from his willingness to open his life for examination. When others questioned his spiritual credentials, he simply reminded them of the high standards of discipleship to which he adhered: "You, however, know all about my teaching, my way of life, my purpose, faith, patience, love, endurance" (2 Tim. 3:10).

Throughout his ministry, Paul had many critics. In the end, however, the critics could not sustain a spiritual charge against him. His life of discipleship defended him and won the case convincingly. As a result, countless people followed Paul and learned how to be better followers of Jesus.

LEADERSHIP IN PHASE TWO FOLLOWING

Communicators often cite this truism: the *medium* is the *message*. They recognize that the way a message is communicated impacts the message itself. The early church understood this concept and linked the *message* with the *messenger*. Paul and the other apostles encouraged people in the New Testament church to monitor the lives of those who aspired to leadership. Lifestyle would always tell the story. If people examined the lives of would-be leaders, they would know if the person was qualified to lead and worthy of being followed. Once again, Paul used his own life as an exemplary model:

> Join with others in following my example, brothers, and take note of those who live according to the pattern we gave you. (Phil. 3:17)

For you yourselves know how you ought to follow our example. . . . We did this, not because we do not have the right to such help, but in order to make ourselves a model for you to follow. (2 Thess. 3:7, 9)

For this reason I am sending to you Timothy, my son whom I love, who is faithful in the Lord. He will remind you of my way of life in Christ Jesus, which agrees with what I teach everywhere in every church. (1 Cor. 4:17)

How should leaders and potential leaders be evaluated? Analyze the pattern of their lives. If their words and their actions over a period of time demonstrate that they are following Christ effectively, then they are worth following. Until a pattern of discipleship develops, however, withhold judgment. Inexperienced or unproven leaders may get you lost.

Guidelines for Today's Spiritual Leaders

The model of spiritual leadership described in the New Testament offers a sound guideline we can use today. All who influence others for Christ can measure their lives by the first-century model. The following checklist serves as a starting point for evaluation:

Follow Christ as your first priority. Your gift to people is the degree to which you help them follow Jesus. If your relationship with Jesus becomes stale and you struggle to follow, you have little to offer others. If you lose sight of Jesus, you lack the essential requirement for Christian leadership. Rather than attempting to lead others, focus your full attention on restoring your relationship as Jesus' disciple.

Never overestimate your strengths or underestimate your weaknesses. Other people may develop unrealistic perceptions of your leadership capabilities. They may inflate your strengths and minimize your weaknesses. If so, refuse to listen to them. Even if no one else is objective, you need to be realistic about who God has equipped you to be and what God has prepared you to do.

Refuse to be "right" all the time. Resist the expectation that you, as the leader, must know everything. That's unrealistic. If you fall into that trap, you will fail. Sometimes you will be right; sometimes you will be wrong. Just because you are an expert on Subject A doesn't mean you have anything to contribute on Subject B. Don't allow followers to make you the final authority on every subject and the last word in every decision.

Admit when you are weak or lost. Attempting to lead when you have no strength, or to guide others when you have no clue where you are going, is pointless. Life is confusing. So why play the "I know the way every time" game in the first place? When you know the way, go ahead and lead. If you don't know the way (for whatever reason), don't fake it.

THE CHALLENGE OF BEING FOLLOWED

In reality, every follower of Christ influences others by word or deed. As a result, we are all leaders whether one person looks to us for guidance or thousands wait for our next directive. Numbers don't change the essential nature of leadership. Having more followers merely multiplies the demands placed on the leader.

When you're being followed, it's important to monitor your reserves—physical, emotional, and spiritual reserves. All need to be used wisely and replenished. Jesus modeled this truth through His actions and in His teaching. By following His example, we can develop some guidelines that help us maintain adequate reserves.

One leader said it well: "You can never do enough for people, if you are always with people." In the midst of profound human need, Jesus often slipped away to spend time alone. For Him, solitude usually came late at night or early in the morning. To achieve that same solitude in our lives, less sleep is frequently the price to be paid. Nonetheless, wise leaders know that time alone is not an option but a necessity. Here are some ways we can keep our reserve levels high:

- Whatever the price, we need time alone with God. Time to be still, to think. Time to refresh our relationship with Him.

- We need time to renew our minds through reading and reflecting on the Scriptures and time to sensitize ourselves to God's presence and direction through prayer.

- Beyond the spiritual, we need time for exercise and periods of rest in order to renew ourselves physically.

▶ We need time for recreation, for friendships, and other activities that refill our emotional tanks.

Other people cannot fill our reserve tanks for us. We are responsible for keeping our tanks full and investing the time required to accomplish the task. Certainly, emergencies come when needs cannot wait. In those situations, we will drain reserves to meet the crisis, but we cannot let life become one perpetual emergency even if people insist that it is. If we develop a pattern of giving without replenishing, we will ultimately face a crisis in our own lives. Once that pattern develops, our crash will come. It's not a question of if; it's only a matter of when.

Your Values and Mission

Once we develop a strategy for keeping our tanks full, we need to be sure we are moving in the right direction in our lives. Take time away from people and ask God to help you answer the following questions:

▶ What has God called you to do? What do you want to do? What can you do that others cannot or will not do?

▶ What do you want more of in your life? What do you want less of in your life?

▶ For what are you willing to exchange your life? How should you live your life now so that when you reach the end, you can look back without regrets?

Life is a jungle, and none of us can afford to get lost in the underbrush. Occasionally, we need to climb a hill and take a longer view, setting our course by the next mountain instead of the next clump of trees. If we fail to order our lives around our relationship with God, others will schedule our lives for us. Handing them our calendars will ensure *busy lives*. Only we can strive for *purposeful lives*.

A Realistic View of People

In spite of adequate reserves and a clear vision, unrealistic expectations about people crush many potential leaders. As we are being followed, we need a realistic picture of human nature. Draw on Jesus' life and His encounters with different types of people. Study your own experiences. Develop a "people map" that helps you anticipate the demands that people will bring to your life.

People will be demanding. Anticipate their interruptions. Don't be surprised when people are self-absorbed and fickle. Prepare to take a stand on principle even as you watch people leave in droves. Manage your disappointment when people let you down. At the same time, never lose sight of the God-given potential that resides in every person. We need to take people as they are and help them progress. Not everyone who follows will become a superstar disciple, but everyone can move forward.

A Heritage of Discipleship

As we struggle to help people God brings into our lives, we can thank God for those who allowed us to follow them. They loved us even when we interrupted. When we called, demanding attention, they invited us to come over. When we were fickle and self-centered, they challenged us to higher standards. Even when we walked away in rebellion, they nurtured a dream for our future and expected us to fulfill it. Many invested in us so we can now invest in others. By God's grace, those who follow us will one day find others following them. In this way, the chain of discipleship continues with ever-expanding influence.

THE WEAK LEADER WHO WAS STRONG

One of the strange truths of the Christian life and leadership is that when we are weak, we are strong because our weakness drives us to depend more fully on Jesus. I heard of one man who embodied this paradox of leadership. One Sunday morning, this pastor stood before his congregation to preach the morning sermon. To the surprise of the waiting crowd, he said, "Friends, I have struggled all week to prepare a sermon. But I now confess that I stand before you empty handed. I am tired. I am confused. I am afraid. All week, I've pleaded with God to give me His message for you. But when I've prayed, I have felt nothing and heard nothing. As your pastor, I want to help you, but my cup is empty and my well is dry. I have nothing to give. I feel like such a failure. I am so sorry."

Then the pastor stepped down from the platform, made his way slowly to the first pew, and sat down. Covering his face with his hands, he began to sob.

How would you have responded? How do you think most congregations would respond? The situation involved no moral failure on the part of this pastor, no shirking of his duties, no irresponsible actions.

The room was quiet, still. Then one person stood and walked to the pastor's side. Kneeling, he placed his hand on the pastor's shoulder and simply began praying. Another person moved to the front, knelt, touched the pastor, and joined the first prayer. More people came until they encircled their pastor. Those who could not reach the front prayed where they were seated. That morning, that church became a safe place for one man. As a leader, he was strong enough to admit he was weak and had enough integrity to admit that he had temporarily lost his way.

Wise leaders step down when they get lost. I expect it was not long before that pastor found his way and led again. When he did, I suspect most people followed him with even greater respect and love.

In the Final Analysis

Even if those who follow place unrealistic expectations on us, the One we follow does not. The psalmist understood this and took comfort in it: "As a father has compassion on his children, so the LORD has compassion on those who fear him; for he knows how we are formed, he remembers that we are dust" (Ps. 103:13–14).

When we are strong, God knows the source of our strength. When we falter, God understands. He knows all about us and continues to love us. In the end, He gives us the strength to stand and lead as well as strength to sit and wait.

What about that "waiting" moment when we are discouraged, tired, and spiritually disoriented? The prophet Isaiah could have said, "Been there; done that!" Perhaps that's why God allowed him to write these words: "Do you not know? Have you not heard? The LORD is the everlasting God, the Creator of the ends of the earth. He will not grow tired or weary, and his understanding no one can fathom. He gives strength to the weary and increases the power of the weak. Even youths grow tired and weary, and young men stumble and fall; but those who hope in the LORD will renew their strength. They will soar on wings like eagles; they will run and not grow weary, they will walk and not be faint" (Isa. 40:28–31).

Those who wait and hope will get up—maybe not immediately but in time. Perhaps then we will see clearly with the perspective of a soaring eagle. Maybe we will run like a marathoner striding toward a distant finish line. At the very least, we will walk—a slow walk the "following" way. That is a good goal for those of us who follow Jesus and want to help others to do the same thing.

THE VALUE
OF STAYING BEHIND

24

*Following Jesus makes
life meaningful.*

As the lights dimmed in the small theater, the audience fidgeted with anticipation and waited for the play to begin. In the darkness, the room filled with the rhythmic sound of a beating heart—"lupdump, lupdump, lupdump." Colored lights cast pale, amorphous shapes on the black curtain that shrouded the stage. The lights grew brighter. The heart beat louder.

The smack of a hand hitting bare flesh startled the audience. A wail—the "oohwah, oohwah" of a newborn baby—rose above the beat of the pounding heart. Then sounds of breathing began. Inhale, exhale. In, then out.

Minutes later with fluid motion the thick curtain rose and revealed a large mound in the center of an otherwise bare stage. Black-clothed and hooded people walked from all sides of the stage with choreographed precision. They clasped the edges of a black tarp covering the mound, raised it quickly, and laid it aside before moving away like shadows. Immediately, the room filled with the stench of a stockyard after a summer rainstorm. The audience stared, startled by the realization that the mound was as it smelled—a huge pile of manure. Theater chairs squeaked, purses snapped, and pocket change jingled as people searched for handkerchiefs to cover their noses. These new sounds added to the cacophony in progress: lupdump, oohwah, inhale, exhale.

Colored spotlights illumined the manure. Gradually, the cry of the baby stopped and the breathing grew stronger and louder. Later, a deep-chest, hacking cough exploded, one choking cough after another, desperate, relentless. The collection of discordant sounds grew louder as the stench of the moist manure filled every sense of those who watched. The lights mesmerized them. The noise hurt their ears. A foul taste accompanied every breath.

Without warning, the coughing stopped and was replaced by a sustained groan. The heart raced while breathing became labored. Another groan. Then a gasp and the breathing stopped. The beating heart began to slow: lupdump, lupdump . . . lupdump . . . lupdump . . . lupdump . . lupdu . . . and then it also stopped.

The curtain closed. The audience sat and then left the theater in absolute silence.

THE ONLY ALTERNATIVE

I finished telling this story and looked across the living room at David and waited for his reaction. Our long weekend together had slowly changed from an extended training session to a comfortable friendship. Since David is an award-winning journalist, I had requested his help in improving my writing. When I first called, he was cordial but stated bluntly that he was not a Christian but thought he could evaluate my writing without getting "hung up" in the content. Then he surprised me by offering his home as the site for our training. When I learned that he and his wife lived in a rugged cabin on fifty acres of land nestled in the coastal rainforest of the Northwest, I was even more excited. It sounded too good to be true: a beautiful setting and time with an exceptional writer.

I had been working on this book for almost a year and gave the completed manuscript to my editor the day before I left for David's cabin. For me, there is no greater satisfaction than completing a long, hard project, so I anticipated my time with David as a celebration and a time to relax. Although I had expected a good teacher-to-student relationship, I was surprised by our easy conversation and budding friendship. We shared our divergent views openly and laughed about the odds of two people like us, as different as we are, ending up together for an extended weekend.

Our time together included wonderful meals, walks in the woods, and stimulating, free-wheeling conversations. It was in that context that I told him the story about the manure pile. When I finished, David sat in his recliner and stared out the wall of windows as the fading light silhouetted the fir trees on the surrounding hills. After a few moments he simply said, "That's just about right."

What? I thought. *Life is a pile of manure?* Really? I was stunned. I had told David the story as a point of contrast to illustrate the importance of my relationship with Christ and the meaning He brings to my life. I knew David was a brilliant man who had spent years articulating questions and searching for the essential answers to life, but in spite of that I was not prepared for his raw response. With one statement, he affirmed my story and stated his conclusion about life.

In the silence that followed, I thought about following Jesus—partially because of my book but more importantly because I saw the stakes more clearly. God's invitation for us to know and follow Him offers the only alternative to David's conclusion. Without it? Well, without that invitation, then David was right. Faith is just a drug we take to dull the painful realities of a manure-pile life we cannot face.

I thought about the completed manuscript waiting with my editor, and a numbing idea filled my mind: I had failed. I had not communicated adequately the importance and privilege of following Jesus. David's comment began a shock wave in my soul that shook until I faced what I did not want to admit. I would need to begin again and rewrite my book.

Emotionally, I was devastated. When I returned home, I discussed the experience with my wife and told her what I needed to do. As always, she supported me. Then I discussed it with my editor, and she encouraged me to "get it right" even if it meant delaying the book for a year. So that is what I have attempted to do.

What you have just read came from that additional year of work. During that year, God helped me understand the Seven-Step Process of Following as I struggled to grasp how following Jesus changes our lives and gives us purpose. I gained new insights into the obstacles that keep us from becoming better followers of Jesus and realized that those obstacles can be identified and avoided. God helped me learn more about Phase Two Following—how we follow a leader we cannot see. Finally, with new conviction, I saw that helping others follow Jesus is the essence of Christian leadership and that we can only help them to the degree that we are following Him ourselves.

In the end, writing this book became a rich experience of following Jesus—a spiritual odyssey that changed and renewed me. Now as I

end the process for the second time, I am overwhelmed with the awareness that our God of grace invites us to know and follow Him. Because
of Jesus, we are not trapped in a mechanistic world governed by mindless evolutionary forces that gut life of meaning, purpose, and hope.
Because of Jesus, we can escape our genetic boxes and become more
than we are. Because of Jesus, we can change and then allow Jesus to
use us to change the world. Because of Jesus, we can make the trip and
learn the way. And then, we can invite others to follow us as we follow
Him.

David was right—except for one thing. Dennis Covington's
description of his childhood and how his father called him home in the
evening helps me picture the spiritual reality.

> It's late afternoon at the lake. The turtles are moving
> closer to shore. The surface of the water is undisturbed, an
> expanse of smooth, gray slate. Most of the children in the
> neighborhood are called home for supper by their mothers.
> They open the back doors, wipe their hands on their aprons
> and yell, "Willie!" or "Joe!" or "Ray!" Either that or they use
> a bell, bolted to the door frame and loud enough to start the
> dogs barking in backyards all along the street. But I was
> always called home by my father, and he didn't do it in the
> customary way. He walked down the alley all the way to the
> lake. If I was close, I could hear his shoes on the gravel before
> he came into sight. If I was far, I would see him across the
> surface of the water, emerging out of shadows and into the
> gray light. He would stand with his hands in the pockets of
> his windbreaker while he looked for me. This is how he got
> me to come home. He always came to the place I was before
> he called my name.[11]

That's what Jesus does for us. He doesn't call us from afar; instead,
He comes down to where we are. He invites us to follow Him home and
allow that experience to transform our lives. We get ahead by staying
behind. The walk home with Jesus changes everything.

REFLECTION QUESTIONS

Chapter One

1. Think of a time you followed someone to a destination that was new to you. What did you do, consciously or unconsciously, that enabled you to follow the leader?
2. See if you can begin to think like a followologist. Use the physical situation you have just described and see if you can discover any principles that you can apply to your spiritual life. If you struggle, don't worry. By the end of this book, you'll make the connection easily and will be surprised by the insights about discipleship you discover.
3. How would you define Followology?

Chapter Two

1. Imagine that you were one of the Israelites following the pillars of cloud and fire through the desert. How do you think you would have responded to that "following system"? Why?
2. What similarities, if any, do you see between the children of Israel's experience of following God through the desert and your current experience of following Jesus?
3. God took the initiative in helping the children of Israel follow Him through the desert. Do you believe God takes the initiative in helping you follow Jesus today? If not, why not? If so, how have you experienced this in your own spiritual life recently?

Chapter Three

1. Review the seven principles in the "following" process. Be sure that you have them clearly in mind before you begin part 2 of our study.
2. Recall a time when you have followed someone over an extended period of time to a destination. See if you can identify each of the seven principles in the "following" process in your experience.
3. After this initial overview of the seven-step "following" process, what implications do you see for your life as Jesus' disciple?

Chapter Four

1. Based on your knowledge of the Old Testament, can you recall situations when God asked people (other than the children of Israel in the desert) to follow Him? See how many individual followers you can identify.
2. "Following was important to Jesus." How would you defend this statement based on the material you have read in this chapter?
3. Before you began your study of Followology, had you focused on "following" as a central priority in discipleship? Has your study so far changed your perspective on "following"? If so, how?

Chapter Five

1. In what ways can you identify with Jesus' twelve disciples?
2. Describe a time when you thought you knew the way and resisted the opportunity to follow a leader or heed advice and then discovered that you really should have listened to that leader. How did your awareness of your need to follow influence your decision to follow?
3. In your spiritual life right now, how aware are you of your need to follow Jesus? How is that awareness affecting your spiritual life?

Chapter Six

1. Recall a time when you were traveling to a destination and followed the wrong leader—someone who did not know the way. When did you realize you were following the wrong leader? How did you feel? What did you do?
2. Before reading this chapter, did you assume that Jesus' disciples decided to follow Him the first time they met Him? If they did in fact spend some time learning more about Jesus before they made their final decision to follow Him, do you consider this encouraging or troublesome? Why?
3. Describe the time when you understood that Jesus was your Lord and you committed your life to follow Him? If you have not done so, why not take that step of faith now?

Chapter Seven

1. How would you describe the importance of "focus" in the process of following?
2. In your spiritual life, what distracts you from following Jesus?
3. If you decided to make your spiritual life a higher priority, what changes would you have to make? How would those changes help you increase your focus on Jesus?

Chapter Eight

1. Is it possible to be a follower if you are not following? Consider the implications of this statement in physical following and then in spiritual following.
2. What unspoken expectations do you have about following Jesus? What conditions have you set for your discipleship? What excuses have you made for not following Jesus with greater commitment?
3. What adjustments do you need to make in your life so you can follow Jesus? Are you ready to make those adjustments? Why or why not?

Chapter Nine

1. Is it easier for you to follow a leader than to follow directions? Why?
2. What words would you use to describe the disciples' relationship with Jesus? Would you use any of those words to describe your relationship with Jesus? Why or why not?
3. How would you rate your relationship with Jesus right now: (1) getting stronger, (2) holding steady, (3) losing ground? How do you want your relationship with Jesus to change?

Chapter Ten

1. When you read about the disciples in the four Gospels, then read about them again in the Book of Acts, do you ever marvel at the degree to which these men changed? How do their experiences of transformation make you feel about your spiritual life?
2. When you read the lyrics to "The Touch of the Master's Hand," what emotions do you feel? Do those words describe your spiritual journey to God and your subsequent growth as a Christian? If so, how?
3. What else do you want God to do in your life as He continues to transform your life? Ask God to touch your life in a special way that reminds you that He is not finished with you yet.

Chapter Eleven

1. Think about a time you made a long trip. How did the nature of the destination change the way you felt about the trip?
2. In what ways does the reality of heaven impact the way you live now? How does the reality of that spiritual destination change the way you view the challenges of discipleship now?
3. Can you picture yourself in the story of "The Runner's Song?" Can you envision yourself running toward your destination alongside Jesus with the sounds of the saints in the stands calling to you with encouragement? Why not memorize Hebrews 12:1-2 and allow that verse to help you keep your eyes on Jesus?

Chapter Twelve

1. Read Mark 1 and imagine that you were with the disciples when they were looking for Jesus. How would you have felt? What would you have said to Jesus?
2. What are some practical ways you struggle with "role confusion" in your relationship with Jesus? What evidence do you see in your life that you have stopped following and started leading?
3. Read this statement aloud: "Jesus is the leader; I am the follower. My goal today is to follow His schedule, accomplish His agenda; reach His destination, and love whoever He sends my way." How would your life change if that statement became the prayer and goal of your heart every day?

Chapter Thirteen

1. To what degree have you had a hot-dog attitude in your spiritual life? If this has been a problem for you, what changes are you planning to make? When? How?
2. In what ways are you seeking to let Christ increase in the eyes of others while you decrease?
3. As a Christian, what is the measure you are using to define "greatness"?

Chapter Fourteen

1. Which of Jesus' disciples are most like you? Which are least like you? Why?
2. To what degree have you focused on other people rather than seeking to become the unique disciple that God intends for you to become?
3. If you followed the B.Y.O.D. principle (be your own disciple), which gifts and abilities in your life do you think God would develop so you could become the best disciple you can be?

Chapter Fifteen

1. When you began following Jesus, were your expectations realistic or unrealistic? Why?
2. How have your expectations about following Jesus changed? Why?

3. How is discipleship "costly" for you? How is it "worth it"? Are those two dimensions of discipleship in balance for you?

Chapter Sixteen
1. In school, how did you feel about tests?
2. What are some of the most significant spiritual tests you have experienced recently? What did you discover about the progress you are making? What did you learn about areas in which you still need to grow?
3. What is your attitude now about spiritual tests? Do you resist them? Do you celebrate them? Or are you somewhere in between.

Chapter Seventeen
1. Can you identify with Peter's failures? If so, how?
2. Do you struggle to believe that God will forgive you and that you can continue to follow Him in spite of your failures? If so, how does Jesus' response to Peter's failure help you deal with your own failure?
3. Are you ready to move beyond your failure and begin following Jesus again with renewed commitment? If so, tell God now and get ready to move on.

Chapter Eighteen
1. Have you ever followed a physical leader you could not see? What made that possible? What spiritual principles can you draw from that experience?
2. If you had been with Jesus' disciples the day He talked about the new phase of following, how would you have responded?
3. Which of the benefits of Phase Two Following do you value the most when compared to the benefits of Phase One Following?
4. As a Phase Two Follower of Jesus, where are you on the continuum between a "CB disciple" and a "cellular disciple"?

Chapter Nineteen

1. To what degree are you using God's Word as the spiritual map to navigate your life? What changes do you need to make to use God's Word more effectively?
2. Describe a time when the Holy Spirit used a particular passage of Scripture to help you make a decision or do the right thing in a certain situation.
3. Do you agree or disagree with this statement: "Each passage of Scripture has one correct interpretation"? Why do you agree or disagree?
4. Some Christians say, "I know that is what the passage says, but this is what it means to me." Would a statement like that bother you? Why or why not?

Chapter Twenty

1. How does God speak to you?
2. Which of the subjective means of communication mentioned in this chapter has God used to speak to you? Which has He used most often?
3. Describe a time when you have sensed God speaking to you through your feelings, opportunities, giftedness, or failures and you then validated what you were hearing with a passage of Scripture. Did the objective voice of Scripture confirm what you were hearing through other subjective means? If so, how did you feel? If not, how did you respond?

Chapter Twenty-One

1. Recall a time you became separated from a leader you knew very well. How did your relationship with that leader enable you to anticipate what he would do? How did that help you find and follow him again?
2. When you feel spiritually disoriented and cannot sense God working in or around your life, how do you seek to find Him? Where do you look for His activity?
3. Which of the "no-brainer" signs of God's work mentioned in this chapter do you use to see Jesus at work around you? What other signs would you add to the list?

Chapter Twenty-Two

1. Can you identify with how Thomas felt after the crucifixion? How do you think he felt when he saw Jesus standing by his side?
2. Have you experienced a time of "discipleship darkness" when you struggled to sense God's presence? What did you learn through that experience?
3. What do you think God teaches us in the darkness that we can learn no other way?

Chapter Twenty-Three

1. Do you think of yourself as a leader? Why or why not?
2. If others follow you, what will they learn about following Jesus? What strengths will they see? What weaknesses will they see?
3. How full are your "reserves" right now? Your physical reserves? Your emotional reserves? Your spiritual reserves? What steps are you taking to keep your reserves full?
4. Who are the people who have helped you follow Jesus? What did they do that helped you focus on Jesus rather than focusing on them?

Chapter Twenty-Four

1. How would you explain to someone how following Jesus makes life meaningful?
2. When did you hear Jesus "call your name" and invite you to follow Him home?
3. How fully are you following Jesus? What changes do you need to make to become a better follower of Jesus? What changes have you decided to make?

NOTES

Chapter Six

1. Johnson M. Cheney and Stanley Ellisen, *The Greatest Story* (Sisters, Oreg.: Multnomah Books, 1994).
2. Based on the article by Terrence Petty, "Hitler's Men: Judgment at Nuremberg," *The Tennessean*, 19 November 1995.

Chapter Nine

3. *Rapid Rail System* (City of Atlanta, effective Date: June 25, 1994).

Chapter Ten

4. John Kramp, "The Touch of the Master's Hand" (The Benson Company, 1980), used by permission.

Chapter Eleven

5. John Kramp, "The Runners Song," © 1981.
6. Joni Eareckson Tada, *Heaven: Your Real Home* (Grand Rapids: Zondervan Publishing House, 1995), 155; used by permission.

Chapter Fifteen

7. John Kramp, "Pennies for Treasures," © 1983.

Chapter Twenty-Two

8. Philip Yancey, "Confessions of a Spiritual Amnesiac," *Christianity Today*, 15 July 1996, 72; used by permission.
9. Philip Yancey, *Disappointment with God* (Grand Rapids: Zondervan Publishing House, 1988).
10. Yancey, "Confessions," 72.

Chapter Twenty-Four

11. Dennis Covington, *Salvation on Sand Mountain* (Reading, Mass.: Addison-Wesley Longman Publishing Company), 239–40; used by permission.

HAVE YOU READ

Out of Their Faces and Into Their Shoes?

Here's what others are saying about this book:

"John Kramp provides many keen insights to help us understand that our motive for evangelism must be the same as the Lord Jesus Christ— love for lost people and relating to them on their level. I highly recommend this helpful book."

Dr. Bill Bright, Founder and President
Campus Crusade for Christ

"All of us are called to Christ's search and rescue mission. Here's a delightful study on a critical subject—the way people get lost and how they can be found. Right on target!"

Dr. Robert E. Coleman
Director,
School of World Mission and Evangelism
Trinity Evangelical Divinity School
Author of *The Master Plan of Evangelism*

"If you've been wanting to tell your friends about Christ, here's how. John Kramp's book brings a most fascinating and unique perspective."

Bill Hybels, Senior Pastor
Willow Creek Community Church

"If you only read one book on evangelism this year, make sure it's this one. John Kramp's fresh and readable approach to sharing your faith is brilliant. This book is terrific."

Dr. Rick Warren, Pastor
Saddleback Valley Community Church
Mission Viejo, California

OUT OF THEIR FACES AND INTO THEIR SHOES

How to Understand Spiritually Lost People and Give Them Directions to God

JOHN KRAMP